Martha Washington

"THIS ELEVATED POSITION…"

A Catalogue And Guide To The National First Ladies' Library
And The Importance Of First Lady History

Edited by
Carl Sferrazza Anthony

Copyright © 2003 by National First Ladies' Library
All rights reserved.

Library of Congress Control Number: 2003095729

ISBN 0-9744566-0-8

Edited by Carl Sferrazza Anthony
Book designed by WRL Advertising — Canton, Ohio

Every effort has been made to verify the accuracy
of the information and give proper credit to
the photographs contained herein. Any errors or
omissions will be corrected in future printings.

TABLE OF CONTENTS

LETTERS FROM THE FIRST LADIES

THE NATIONAL FIRST LADIES' LIBRARY

FIRST LADY HISTORY, by Carl Sferrazza Anthony

LETTERS FROM THE FIRST LADIES

Stonewall, Texas

THE WHITE HOUSE HAS MANY MEMORIES FOR ME, SOME OF THEM SAD, MORE OF THEM JOYOUS. BUT TOWERING OVER ALL OF THEM IS THE CONSTANT SOURCE OF A HOST OF COMPANIONS.

WHENEVER I WALKED THROUGH ITS ROOMS, I KNEW THAT I WALKED WITH HISTORY – THE LONG LINE OF PRESIDENTS AND THEIR WIVES AND THEIR CHILDREN WHO HAD OCCUPIED THIS HOUSE. EACH FAMILY HAS LEFT SOMETHING OF ITSELF THERE, THROUGH SOME MATERIAL CHANGE, MORE ESPECIALLY THROUGH SOME TOUCH OF THE INDIVIDUAL HUMAN SPIRIT.

THE CONSTITUTION OF THE UNITED STATES DOES NOT MENTION THE FIRST LADY. SHE IS ELECTED BY ONE MAN ONLY. THE STATUTE BOOKS ASSIGN HER NO DUTIES; AND YET, WHEN SHE GETS THE JOB, A PODIUM IS THERE IF SHE CARES TO USE IT. I DID.

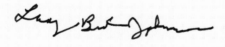

Elizabeth B. Ford

December 9, 2002

Dear Mary,

It is with great admiration and appreciation that I offer my congratulations to the completion of your long held-vision for a national First Ladies Library.

During my own tenure in the White House, our nation celebrated its Bicentennial and at that time, I recall, there was a great resurgence in interest in the contributions of women to the American Revolution. Martha Washington, as her husband's loyal companion and supporter, and Abigail Adams, as her husband's political advisor, were finally being fully appreciated. At that time, the White House Historical Association also issued its first edition of a book on the First Ladies. The work that you and the National First Ladies Library are planning to do in your new research center and library facility shall continue in this relatively new tradition of documenting the lives and influences of the presidential spouses. It will contribute to an overall appreciation of our American culture.

When I reflect upon my own personal experience with breast cancer in September of 1974, I am reminded of just how great an impact a First lady can have. News cameras kept a vigil outside the hospital. On the television news was coverage of thousands of American women lining up for early breast cancer detection. It suddenly hit me just how much of an international platform a First lady can have to do good, to initiate improvements and to help others – if she chooses to do so.

Best Wishes,

Betty Ford

Ms. Mary Regula
President, National First Ladies Library
331 Market Avenue South
Canton, Ohio 44702-2107

ROSALYNN CARTER

ROSALYNN CARTER

24 January 2003

Dear Friends,

Being first lady of the United States is a wonderful opportunity and a daunting challenge. The wife of the president unquestionably wields substantial power and influence, yet since she has no "official" title, she also enjoys a special freedom to tailor her role to suit herself.

Historically presidents' spouses had been expected to limit their duties to service as adoring wives, perfect mothers, and hostesses beyond compare, but beginning most notably with Eleanor Roosevelt, who used her position and visibility to call attention to injustice and need, many modern first ladies have been compelled to become actively involved in advancing their own particular areas of interest. These interests have included the restoration of the White House, the beautification of America, the Equal Rights Amendment, treatment and services for mentally ill people, the war on drugs, literacy, health care reform, and education. First ladies' contributions to our nation's culture and society are significant, and our influence is not limited to a four- or eight-year term. For the rest of her life, a first lady can be a tremendous advocate for whatever causes she chooses. As a public figure, her access to the media is an important resource she can use either to highlight great achievements and service or to expose dire circumstances and intolerable wrongdoing.

It is not easy to be the first lady, with every move subject to the most detailed scrutiny and often criticism. You have to learn to ignore any hurtful words and do what you know to be right for your husband, your family, your cause, and your country.

I was deeply honored to serve as first lady. Early on, I recognized the huge responsibility it entailed, and I still consider it my duty and joyous obligation to take full advantage of the opportunity. By electing my husband president, the American people blessed me with a mission to try to be a force for good in this world.

Sincerely,

Rosalynn Carter

National First Ladies Library
331 Market Avenue South
Canton, Ohio   44702-2107

OFFICE OF NANCY REAGAN

Dear Friends,

Next to marrying Ronald Reagan fifty years ago and having my children,
serving as First Lady for eight years was the highlight of my life. I will always
be grateful for the opportunity to represent the United States at home and
abroad, to reside for eight years in America's home, and to have had a platform
on which to raise critical issues about which I felt passionate. Those eight
years were a gift I will cherish all the days of my life.

When I arrived in Washington in 1981, I thought I understood the demands
and pressures of being a first lady. After all, I had been First Lady of
California for eight years and was used to living life on display. But, nothing,
and I mean nothing, prepares you for being First Lady of the United States.
It's a singular journey from the very first moment your husband takes the oath
of office. Of course being First Lady teaches you so much - about yourself
and your capacity to serve. It was during those eight years that I found out
what was really important to me. I learned how to help others and, despite the
intense scrutiny, stay true to myself.

While a first lady's most important duty is to love and support her husband,
The President, each of us left our own legacy, interpreting the role to suit our
own personal style and interests. That is why the National First Ladies
Library and Research Center is so useful. Visitors can come to hear stories of
women from diverse backgrounds who, like their husbands, dedicated
themselves to serving their country. I encourage everyone to visit this special
place, and am deeply touched to be a part of it.

President Reagan joins me in sending you our best wishes as you realize your
dream.

Sincerely,

Nancy Reagan

Barbara Bush

January 28, 2003

Dear Friends,

Being the First Lady is the greatest job in the world. As First Lady, I was privileged to meet musicians, painters, athletes, leaders of education and industry, not to mention heads of state from countries all around the globe—the best, most accomplished people in the world.

Lady Bird Johnson said that the First Lady has a bully pulpit to accomplish so much to help people, and that was one of the things I enjoyed most about the job. You have the opportunity to make a difference in so many lives and in the nation itself.

I learned so much during my years as the First Lady, and I will always be grateful for them. It was truly an experience like no other.

With fond memories,

Warmly,

Barbara Bush

Besides marrying the greatest man in the world – I am the luckiest person in the world! ☺

May 2003

Dear Friends,

It gives me great pleasure to serve as an Honorary Chair of the National First Ladies' Library and to contribute to this catalogue and guide.

I will always be grateful for the honor of being First Lady and for the opportunity to serve the President and my country. I was able to advocate for policies and programs that meant the most to me, especially those affecting children and their families, and to do so on a world stage. Added to this was the privilege of living in the White House, to preserve its historical integrity, to host a grand celebration of the new Millennium, and in eight years, welcome millions of visitors from all over the world. I had the opportunity also to represent our nation in the capitals of Europe, in the developing world, and in emerging democracies where our tradition of representative government is envied and revered. I will always treasure these, and many other extraordinary experiences and opportunities, that only a First Lady may enjoy.

The Library, with its education and research center, is a truly unique venue for learning the rich history of our first ladies and through them examining the presidency and the social and political history of our nation. I hope you will enjoy your visit and leave the Library with a new appreciation for the important role our first ladies have played in the life of our nation.

With best wishes, I am

Sincerely yours,

Hillary Rodham Clinton

THE WHITE HOUSE

WASHINGTON

March 2, 2003

Dear Friends,

The resources of the National First Ladies Library are wonderful, and I hope you will find yourself drawn into the life and times of each of the presidential wives as I have been. The grace and grit of my predecessors are always an inspiration to me.

Since September 11, 2001, I often think of Dolley Madison, whose quick thinking saved the incomparable Gilbert Stuart portrait of George Washington from burning with the White House during the War of 1812; or Mary Todd Lincoln, who with her husband faced the national darkness of civil war and the personal darkness of their adored little Willie's death; or Eleanor Roosevelt, who walked these halls by her husband's side during difficult times and became an advocate for many Americans who had no voice.

And of course, the First Lady I think of most and love best, whose strength, humor and wisdom encourage me every day, is my own mother-in-law Barbara Bush. Her continuing work for literacy in the United States is a great example of the good that can be accomplished through the opportunities afforded to each president's spouse.

Because I was a teacher and a librarian, one of my strongest beliefs is that every child in America must read as well as possible and have excellent teachers. I am grateful to be able to gather the best research and most successful programs for reading and teacher recruitment and help spread them throughout the country. I am also participating in education efforts on a worldwide basis as the official Goodwill Ambassador for the United Nations Educational, Scientific and Cultural Organization's Decade of Literacy.

The chance to work on a national and international level for causes I believe in is a gift. And the chance to do that work by the side of the man I believe in is the best gift of all.

Sincerely,

Laura Bush

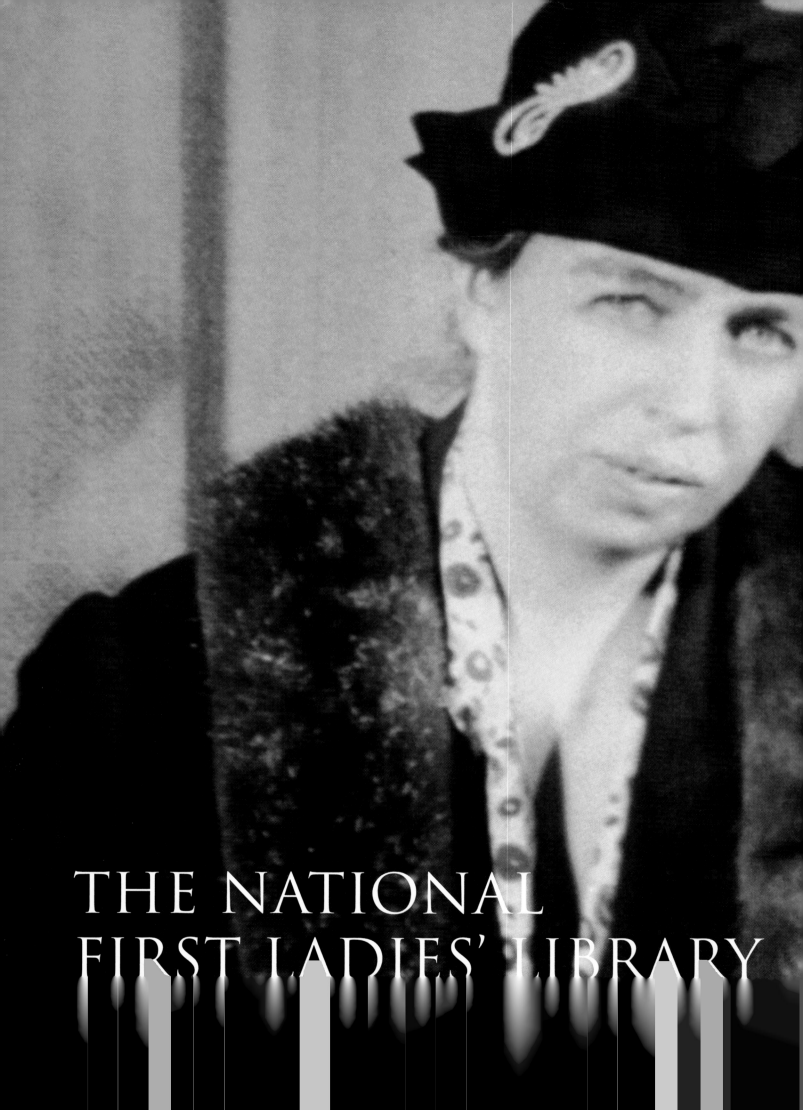

THE NATIONAL
FIRST LADIES' LIBRARY

HOW IT CAME TO BE

By Mary Regula, Founder and President of the National First Ladies' Library

> "When you cease to make a contribution,
>
> you begin to die."

Eleanor Roosevelt
Letter to Mr. Horne / Feb. 19, 1960

Although I did not realize it until recently, the creation of the National First Ladies' Library was long in the making. And, in retrospect, it seems that so many of my experiences were leading up to it.

I am the daughter of immigrant parents, and I always wanted to be an all-American woman. It wasn't that my mother wasn't a magnificent and, in her way, a heroic role model. I just wanted to be more than a mother and homemaker, and I tended to look for role models who led more exciting and interesting lives.

I loved reading because I had a voracious appetite for information about American life. When I was a little girl and then a student of the public school system in the 1940s in Girard, Ohio, a steel mill town, there were no women role models in American history for me to emulate. The history books most American children used at the time never mentioned any women of achievement except the "heroines" who were caught in the midst of war – Clara Barton, "the nurse" who tended to the Union wounded of the Civil War, (who happened to found the Red Cross) or Molly Pitcher who had "a cannonball rip her dress," while she was bringing pitchers of water to American Revolutionary soldiers. I knew Joan of Arc had courage to stand up for her beliefs, though she was even further removed in the midst of medieval European history.

But there was quite a woman making history right then and there.

Mary Regula and her mother

I didn't always know exactly what the latest branch of government that the First Lady was "meddling in" but I did remember the strong, sometimes negative reaction many adults seemed to have about Eleanor Roosevelt. But to me - reading her column in the papers during the week, seeing her in newsreels at Saturday matinees at the movies, and hearing her on Sunday nights on the radio – she became one of my ideal women. Not that I in any way consciously emulated her ways, but she was an inspiration, a sign that a woman could be a wife and mother and still pursue her own callings. That a woman could fulfill different roles – sometimes with difficulty and conflict – and yet, in the end, do, as Lady Bird Johnson says, "make my heart sing."

In school, I hadn't really thought about First Ladies as a concept. Martha's husband, George Washington, was the only face looking down from the schoolhouse wall. There were factory-manufactured chairs named for Dolley Madison – always incorrectly spelled as "Dolly" – but I did not know who she was. There were popcorn, ice cream, cake, powder, and lipstick company brands labeled with her name and often her cameo profile. As for Mary Lincoln, if anyone knew anything about her it was that she had "gone crazy" after her husband's assassination.

No, what impressed me was not that Mrs. Roosevelt was a First Lady

Eleanor Roosevelt at radio (pages 16-17) My first exposure to a First Lady was listening to Mrs. Roosevelt's Sunday evening radio show. I knew her voice before I knew what she even looked like. And I admired her.

but that she was just being herself. Somehow I found it great that the wife of a President was speaking her own mind, even if she disagreed with her husband. I remember being very much drawn to the way she had both a maternal instinct in looking after the well-being of soldiers during World War II and a steely toughness in being openly involved in political debate. There was also great support for the Roosevelts in my community. Girard was located in a very Democrat area of Ohio, and everyone in my neighborhood admired Mrs. Roosevelt.

I could only read about the places that Mrs. Roosevelt went to, but I often felt transported nevertheless. Reading became my passion early on in life. As a young person I often went into the adult section of the library to take out books - only to be told that I was not old enough. Still, the library became perhaps the most important place for me. I was especially careful never to damage any books. I revered them. I understood their value. They opened up new worlds to me, truly my window to the world of adventure and romance. Although Youngstown isn't really that far from Girard, going there meant a big trip for us; yet reading allowed me to travel everywhere and anywhere with my mind. My high school English literature teacher took notice of my love of reading and told me, "You need to go to college." She helped me obtain a scholarship to Mount Union College in Alliance, Ohio.

At college I thought I might want to go into some kind of social work, perhaps nursing. After an emergency appendectomy, I realized hospitals were not for me. It was a history teacher, however, who led me down another path simply by the inspiration of his teaching. From those earlier years when I had been looking for women role models, a natural draw to history emerged. Bess Truman was now in the White House, but she never captured my attention. History did, however. It became my major.

It was in college that I met and began dating Ralph Regula. With his education, he was thinking of going to law school. His encouragement led me to earn a teaching degree. It was the first time I met someone who felt as strongly about his beliefs as I did about mine, and he was the first truly live Republican I had ever met. After college I taught social studies in high school, and then taught elementary and middle school for a short time before we married and started a family. At those levels, one teaches a variety of subjects.

When I stopped teaching and we began our family, most of my waking hours were spent rearing three children. I hadn't, however, lost my passion for reading. I was constantly reading stories to the children, and for myself, like many wives and mothers of the era, I joined the Book-of-the-Month Club. And I nearly always chose history books. Historical figures absolutely fascinated me whether they were from English, French or American history. I began to find myself particularly drawn to the Victorian era. From studying that period came a growing interest in the Civil War and, inevitably, an avid curiosity about Abraham Lincoln and the influences that shaped him. It was while reading a memoir of Lincoln written by his former law partner, William Herndon, that the character of Mary Todd Lincoln first captured my attention. Herndon described her in harsh and cruel terms. He suggested that

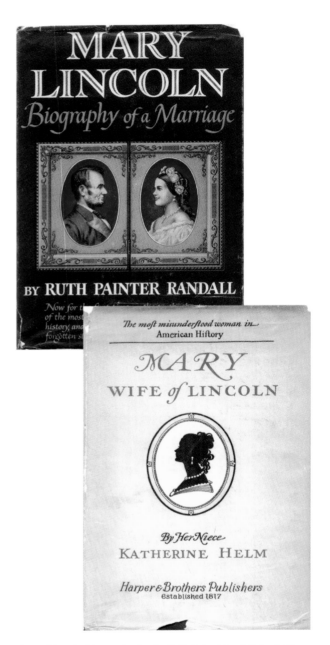

Mary Lincoln biography by Ruth Painter Randall (top), **Mary Lincoln book by Katherine Helm** (bottom). When I was asked to make a Lincoln Day speech and decided to talk on his wife, I initially found a dearth of information. In time, I finally came across two excellent – but quite different – books of Mary Todd Lincoln, one a family memoir by her niece, another a well-documented biography. Both are now in our library.

Mary Regula and Betty Ford When my husband first came to Congress, in 1973, Gerald Ford was still serving as House Minority Leader. As a Congressional wife, I first met Betty Ford. Within a year, she had become Vice President's wife and then, suddenly, due to Nixon's resignation, First Lady. She is seen here several years later when, as president of the Congressional Club, I invited her to come and address the group she herself had belonged to for many years.

Mary Regula and Nancy Reagan When Nancy Reagan became First Lady, I found myself in great empathy with her remark that many political spouses can spot those trying to "end-run" their spouse. I also found myself defending her protectiveness towards President Reagan – and began to search more deeply for the historical context of how her predecessors shaped their role.

she had been nothing but a negative force in Lincoln's life and that he had succeeded in spite of her. Somehow, instinctively, I didn't quite believe this – but I had many more practical obligations at the time than to research the life of Mary Lincoln and defend her.

During the 1950s, Mamie Eisenhower had been in the White House; I remember her as a grandmotherly figure, but she otherwise left no lingering impression on me. Jacqueline Kennedy was different. She was the first First Lady since Eleanor Roosevelt who caught my attention for being so individualistic. The most obvious difference about her was a shining glamour. It seemed that every young woman in the country wanted to copy her suits and hats and gowns, and I was no exception. Still, I had no particular interest in First Ladies. My attention lay closer to home.

Like Jackie Kennedy and most young mothers of that era, my primary responsibilities were the children and the home. Ralph went on to be elected to the state house of representatives and then the state senate. As my children matured, I became involved in activities outside the home. Just at the time of Lady Bird Johnson's beautification campaign, I belonged to a local garden club and so her efforts were naturally of great interest to me. I also became aware of a remarkable woman in Canton, Louise Timken. During World War II, she had been one of a small number of women pilots who ferried airplanes across the ocean to the front. Hers was yet another story of a woman doing the unexpected. It was just about that time that I began to clip and save articles I came across on notable women in American history and contemporary life.

Meanwhile, in the state senate, Ralph was interested in the preservation of the Ohio and Erie Canal that went from Cleveland to Portsmouth. He gave numerous speeches on its historical value and, with the support of the Ohio Legislature, got the state to hold this ribbon of wilderness that ran through the state from being developed. His interest in the project spurred my own curiosity on the history of the canal. I soon began doing independent research on how it changed Ohio, and the men who worked on it – and the women behind them. I put it all together for a speech, "Romance of the Ohio and Erie Canal," and not only Ralph but also I was soon lecturing on the subject to different local and state groups. He was scheduled to speak on Abraham Lincoln at a Lion's Club about this time, but when senate business tied up his schedule, he asked me fill in for him. "You read all those books on the Civil War, you can talk about Lincoln." I would talk – but not about Abraham.

Ever since reading that Herndon book, Mary Lincoln had stayed with me. My clipping file on women's history was quite substantial by this time, but I found nothing on her in it. No problem, I thought, I'll just pick up books on her at the library. There were dozens of books on President Lincoln in the libraries in Canton and nearby Massillon, but very little on his wife. In the short term, I managed to glean enough from the books on Lincoln to patch together a short speech on Mary Todd. In time, I came across two or three young adult books on her, none of which went into much depth nor had much in the way of documentation. Only later did I find some substantive works on her.

It was then that I began to look into general books on the First Ladies, collective biographies where there might be more information on Mrs. Lincoln. There were very few of these and many of them that were written were romanticized. At the time there were no scholarly or definitive biographies of any First Ladies – not even Abigail Adams or Eleanor Roosevelt. I was a bit shocked at the dearth of information. Meanwhile, I began to lecture on Mrs. Lincoln at numerous organizations, clubs and history classes, sometimes in period costume. The most compelling result was that the only aspect of her life that many people recalled was that she was "crazy," a reference to her having been declared insane later in life by what I always considered to be a prejudiced jury. Nobody knew anything about her rabid abolitionist views and how she might have influenced Lincoln in this respect, or her political acumen and judicial observations of Cabinet members and military leaders.

I soon had an opportunity to observe a First Lady first hand. In 1972, midway through Ralph's second term in the state senate, he was elected to Congress. Watergate was in full swing when I first met Pat Nixon, and her husband was under siege. Observing her, I thought she was the most perfect woman I had ever seen – even the seams on her hose were straight! She seemed almost doll-like. It wasn't until we actually met, and she noticed a pin that I was wearing that I saw her warmly come to life and drop the public mask. It was an interesting lesson in how different a public persona can be from a real person – and that there was usually much more to a First Lady than met the eye. Going through the White House during a Christmas party, I had assumed the White House looked the way it did because of Jackie Kennedy's famous restoration. Only later did I discover that Pat Nixon had obtained the majority of Americana in those rooms and had also opened the house to the handicapped and blind, and even saw to it that guide brochures were printed in different languages for those who didn't read English.

I knew Betty Ford better, since Ralph had come to Congress and worked with Jerry Ford, then the House Minority leader. I wholeheartedly

THE WHITE HOUSE

September 11, 1990

It is a great pleasure for me to send heartfelt greetings to all attending the Salute to Mary Regula, given by the Western Stark County Women's Republican Club.

I'm sure that all of you present can bear witness to the many contributions to the life of the community which Mary has unstintingly given. Her tireless efforts, her spirit of optimism, her seemingly endless energy for many worthy causes, have been an inspiration to all of us. Added to that, she is a friend. We all have reason to be grateful to Mary Regula for her dedication and commitment.

Our nation is a better one for having you in it. God bless you!

Warmly,

Barbara Bush

Barbara Bush letter to Mary Regula (top), **Mary Regula and Barbara Bush** (bottom) I always found Barbara Bush to be accessible and humorous. When she came to the Congressional Club in 1989 and I introduced her as "First Lady," she said, "No, just Barbara."

Mary Regula speaking in East Room (top), **Hillary Clinton accessing website in East Room** (middle), **Martha Regula, Mary Regula, Hillary Clinton and Ralph Regula** (bottom) With her own knowledge of First Lady history, Hillary Clinton immediately understood the need I saw for creating a national bibliography on the subject. With her enthusiastic support, we finally created one. It was my daughter Martha who urged me not to publish such a resource, but rather to make it available nationwide through the Internet. All along the way, my husband the Congressman was the most enthusiastic and vital support to making the vision a reality. On February 23, 1998, in an East Room ceremony, the First Lady officially opened the website, accessing her own site.

admired her for being so honest about her breast cancer and the many issues she weighed in on. Equally, I thought that Rosalynn Carter did a great thing when she decided to sit in on Cabinet meetings and take notes on the progress of Carter Administration legislation, so she could speak intelligently to the public. "I've earned my right to be here," she said, and I believed she had, considering all the effort and work she had put into her husband's political rise. In Washington, as a member of the International Club, I also came to know Barbara Bush, who had returned from her life in China, where George had served as chief U.S. liaison. I liked her casualness and honest quality. During the Ford and Carter years, I took note of how much more frequently the media covered the First Ladies and the issues they raised. It was the first generation to benefit from the women's movement, which I had absolutely supported. Although in the Sixties, I was still focused on rearing my children, I believed strongly in the fight for freedom and equality for women in all aspects of American life. I remember being disgusted at the efforts of some to depict "feminists" as some sort of wild women out to destroy society. Another aspect of life in Washington that stirred my awareness was the heavy coverage in the local newspapers there about the activities of women in politics and political wives – other than First Ladies. I remember distinctly a profile of Ambassador Clare Booth Luce. Finally, I thought, a real role model for women.

When Nancy Reagan was being attacked for her protection of the President from those she thought were using him for their own purposes, I felt I could directly relate. My experience has been that women in politics can sometimes recognize frauds or those seeking to make inroads to achieve their own agenda much faster than men can. I vigorously defended Mrs. Reagan's actions in the aftermath of the Iran-Contra scandal when she sought to oust Chief of Staff Don Regan. And, finally, the President did get rid of Regan. I found that I was tending to defend women and First Ladies in such controversies, but I wanted more information on them to make my points. I revisited my earlier efforts to find out more about the lives of past First Ladies. By this time several well researched and written individual and collective biographies about First Ladies had been published. I delved into them with intensity. Oftentimes I came up from the pages discovering whole new aspects of these women's lives – that Martha Washington had been like a business manager at Mount Vernon, or that Eleanor Roosevelt lobbied for legislation or that Julia Grant had weighed in on political appointments. Why hadn't this material been

published previously? And why did so many people still know nothing about this?

With Hillary Clinton's tenure as First Lady, the issue of how much a presidential spouse can influence history was front and center on the national radar screen. I was now searching the Library of Congress and other research centers to find a definitive bibliography that took into account all of the primary and secondary sources available on First Ladies. To my disbelief, there was none. My daughter Martha was by now pursuing her master's in library science and I told her that just such a bibliography needed to be published. "No, mother. It needs to be a website, on the Internet. That way people all over the world could access it." That was the clarion call.

I called together thirteen women in the Canton area to raise money to create this first-of-a-kind comprehensive First Ladies bibliography. They were not a group of social friends; they were all activists in their own right. But it was the support from one woman that turned the local project into a national one. On January 13, 1995, Hillary Clinton welcomed me into her office, and I told her about the idea of the bibliography and, eventually, some sort of library where all of the books and other sources listed could be gathered. "I know exactly what you mean," she said about documenting the First Ladies' lives and contributions, "There is a void." I was impressed by how informed and interested this First Lady was about First Lady history. She not only recommended the person who spent a year creating the bibliography of 40,000+ entries, historian Carl Sferrazza Anthony, but she also agreed to serve as honorary chairman of the effort. All of her living predecessors followed suit, signing on as honorary chairs.

Mary Regula, Rosalynn Carter, Frances Glendening, Sheila Fisher, dedication of Saxton House On June 8, 1998, former First Lady Rosalynn Carter came to Canton to officially cut the ribbon opening the restored Saxton-McKinley House. She has been a generous and enthusiastic supporter from the start.

Simultaneous to this was Ralph's effort in helping to save an old, crumbling building in Canton, about to be torn down. It stood starkly on the corner of Market Avenue and Fourth Street, covered with all sorts of insulation and bric-a-brac. It had been a tavern and a boarding house. It had also been the family home of a youthful Ida Saxton, who later married William McKinley. Although President McKinley had lived in Canton and campaigned in 1896 and 1900 from another front porch there, that structure was destroyed. The Saxton House, where he and Ida had lived for 14 years while he served in Congress, is the only standing structure that the 25th U.S. President called home.

Marsh Belden, Sr., a grandson of Ida McKinley's sister, saved the Saxton House from the wrecking ball. Mr. Belden restored the exterior of the house and had it placed on the National Historic Register. Because of its historical significance, Ralph, as chairman of the Interior subcommittee of Appropriations, brokered an agreement between the National Park Service and the Stark Community Foundation to restore the interior, using it as office space for the Foundation. Ralph insisted that certain historic rooms be open to the public – the main parlor, the ballroom and McKinley's office room. The Foundation redid the interiors in a Federal Style. The National Park Service leased the home to the Foundation.

Our committee was using the house to hold our meetings, but all I had thought we would need was one room with a computer and perhaps a bookcase for the trickle of the old First Lady books and biographies that our committee was beginning to pick up here and there. Restoring the historic rooms was a task we had not anticipated. With the realization that a library was indeed taking shape, we further expanded. In September of 1997, we incorporated in the District of Columbia as the National First Ladies' Library. Besides the local site committee, a national board of directors and national advisory board were named. That same month, Marsh Belden, Jr. offered to donate the 1895 City National Bank Building, a beautiful seven-story Victorian office building, for future expansion. It is located just one block up Market Street from the Saxton-McKinley House. By now a full-fledged effort was underway to collect the thousands of titles of books and articles listed in the completed bibliography. On February 23, 1998 the National First Ladies' Library bibliography website was officially unveiled in the East Room of the White House by Hillary Clinton. The First Lady made the first "hit" on the website when she accessed her own bibliographic records.

With the National First Ladies' Library having so rapidly expanded not only its mission but also accumulation of books and other materials, we entirely engulfed the Saxton-McKinley House. Six months later, on June 8, Ida McKinley's and Barbara Bush's birthday, former First Lady Rosalynn Carter officially dedicated the National First Ladies' Library. In a short period of time (3 years), our committee, through corporate, foundation and individual contributions had raised over $5 million without government funds. It was an idea whose time had come.

The First Ladies Salute First Women awards ceremony was initiated in 1999 to recognize living women who were first in their fields or pioneers in

Hillary Clinton in hallway of Saxton-McKinley House Hillary Clinton continued her strong support of the National First Ladies' Library by helping to make it one of the institutions aided by her Save America's Treasures program. She is seen here on July 23, 1999, the day she came to Canton to make the announcement in the hallway of the Saxton-McKinley House.

their fields. It became our major fundraising source, held in Washington, D.C. It was our second mission goal to educate Americans on the importance of women in our nation's history.

In less than a year, in May of 1999, the Library accepted the donation of the City National Bank as part of its future site. Two months later, First Lady Hillary Clinton came to the library and announced that the old bank building, to be renovated as the National First Ladies' Library Education and Research Center, had been made an "official project" of Save America's Treasures, a millennium project of the President and Mrs. Clinton. By the first month of the new century, the library was notified that it would receive a $2.5 million Save America's Treasures matching grant. Finally, on October 20, 2000, President Clinton signed a bill establishing the First Ladies National Historic Site. Now, the library would operate and manage the Saxton-McKinley House under a cooperative agreement with the National Park Service, with the provision that the future Library Education and Research Center would be donated to the National Park Service and made part of the national historic site.

It may have taken a lifetime to come up with the idea of the library, but once it was there, everything seemed to unfold quickly. Now I find myself looking at a state-of-the-art research facility and library, and a beautifully restored Victorian museum. If someone is searching for a role model, researching a speech or defending a maligned First Lady, there is finally a place where they can come to document the truth. This will become a home for scholars, students, authors and historians alike to finally fill the void in American history.

My favorite inspirational saying is, "Whatever you can do or dream you can, begin it. Action has truth, power and magic in it." It has certainly been my motto in establishing the library for future generations.

Mary Regula, President Bush, Mrs. Bush, Ralph Regula As a former librarian, First Lady Laura Bush had such a strong sense of the importance of a library to a community that she successfully helped lobby for increased federal funding for public libraries all across the nation in 2003, for the 2004 budget.

THE SAXTON HOUSE AND ITS RESTORATION

by Sheila A. Fisher, Ph.D., Vice President of The National First Ladies' Library

> I wish we were not going away from home…
>
> Ida McKinley

Front of Saxton-McKinley House as it looks today (top), **Front of Saxton-McKinley House as it looked in the 19th century** (middle), **Front of Saxton-McKinley House as it looked in 1980s** (bottom) The Saxton House was built in two parts, the first being constructed in the 1840s by Ida Saxton McKinley's maternal grandfather. Seen here as it looked in the 19th century, it deteriorated once it left the ownership of the family. By the 1980s, although it had been saved from destruction when Saxton descendant Marshall Belden, Sr. purchased it, it remained in disrepair. Today, after its thorough interior and exterior restoration and renovation, it looks much as it once did, now serving as the National First Ladies' Library.

The Saxton House was the family home of First Lady Ida Saxton McKinley, wife of our 25th President, William McKinley. Now, this is the magnificently restored home of the First Ladies National Historic Site, which is operated and managed by the National First Ladies' Library.

The Saxton House was built in several sections. The first, primarily the rear section of the house, was built about 1840 by Ida McKinley's maternal grandfather George DeWalt, a pioneer of Canton. Ida's mother, Katherine DeWalt, married James A. Saxton, son of John Saxton, the founder of the Canton Repository, on August 31, 1846. They had three children: Ida, Mary and George. Their oldest child, Ida, was born in Canton on June 8, 1847. The Saxton House was left to James and Katherine Saxton by Ida's grandmother DeWalt in her will in 1869. Sometime thereafter, the Saxtons, along with their three children, moved into the Saxton House, where they lived with Grandfather DeWalt. Ida's father added the front section to the house around 1870.

Ida Saxton had a privileged childhood, her father being a wealthy banker and businessman. She attended local public schools and then private schools in Cleveland and Delhi, New York. Indulged in every whim, she dressed in the finest clothes and was sent to Brooke Hall Seminary boarding school in Media, Pennsylvania in 1866. Ida was bright, quick and beautiful. In 1869, she made a six-month tour of Europe with her sister and a chaperone, exploring Ireland, Scotland, England, Holland, Belgium, France, Germany, Austria, Switzerland and Italy. Upon her return, she worked in her father's bank, the Stark County Bank. Beginning as a clerk, she was then promoted to a cashier and served as bank manager in her father's absence. Although she and Major William McKinley, a Civil War veteran and rising lawyer in town, had earlier met they only began courting after her return from Europe. They married in 1871. The newlyweds moved several blocks north on Market Street from the Saxton House into a wood-frame home given to them as a gift from her father.

At the end of their first year of marriage, Ida gave birth to a daughter, named Kate for her mother. Mrs. Saxton died suddenly on March 14, 1873 which caused Ida to go into a deep depression. She gave birth prematurely to her second daughter, Ida, on April 1, 1873. Little Ida died on August 22, 1873. It was, however, the death of Katie at the age of 3, on June 25, 1875, that broke Ida's health.

For the rest of her life, Ida McKinley would be an invalid, beset by physical and psychological weaknesses. She developed epilepsy, a condition that was not understood in those days. Its victims were often stigmatized by society. Therefore, the details of Ida's illness were never made public. Despite Ida's poor health, her intense love for her husband led her to interest herself in the issues that faced him as he became involved in politics.

McKinley was elected to the U.S. Congress in 1877. The couple leased, then later sold, their home on North Market Street and moved to a residential hotel suite in Washington, D.C. During their summer and holiday breaks or on any visits back to Canton, however, they lived in the Saxton House. Ida's father died in 1887, and McKinley lost his seat in Congress in the 1890 election. Following his 1891 election as Governor, the McKinleys moved to Columbus in the spring of 1892.

In 1895, at the end of his second term as governor, McKinley discovered that the house that Mr. Saxton had bought for him and Ida as a wedding gift was available for rent. Knowing he was going to be running for President that year, and seeking to prove that Ida's health would not be a deterrent in any way, McKinley leased the old house, over which Ida would preside, and began plans for the building of a wide front porch. In February 1896, the couple hosted a mammoth silver wedding anniversary party there, inviting most of Ohio's prominent citizens. This anniversary party was an attempt to show Ida as capable and to allay any rumors of ill health. It was from this house – most notably the front porch – that McKinley's famous Canton campaign was conducted. With his election to the presidency and 1897 inauguration, the McKinleys made the White House their home.

Despite her poor health, Ida McKinley made a definitive impression on the political landscape of turn-of-the-century America. Since the public was never explicitly told the truth about her illnesses, rumor ran rampant during McKinley's first presidential campaign. Consequently, her husband's advisors decided to release the first campaign biography ever printed about a candidate's wife, Sketch of the Life of Mrs. William McKinley, written by Josiah Hartzell. Despite the fact that women did not yet have universal suffrage, the Republican Party frequently made reference to the wives of their potential presidential candidates. They used them as symbols of the candidates' domestic stability. Ida McKinley was a popular symbol in that campaign, and there were buttons and ribbons manufactured that used her image.

As First Lady, there is also great evidence of her keen political perceptions, often identifying opportunists and blocking the appointment of one man ambitious to be the President's military aide. Her trust of White House physician General Leonard Wood was a factor in his being named as commander of the American forces in Cuba in 1898. She also helped a member of the Daughters of the American Revolution obtain a prominent position on a government commission dealing with Philippines matters. Most importantly, however, was her influence on the President after the United States defeated Spain in the Spanish-American War. The First Lady was fixated on the need for Christian missionary work in the islands, to convert the isolated tribes of the northern Luzon territory. According to President McKinley's military aide, Benjamin Montgomery, Ida McKinley's "incessant talk on the conversion of the islanders influenced the President's decision to retain the Philippines." [1]

Ida's ne'er do' well brother George, who never married, continued to live at the Saxton House with the Barbers during the McKinley presidency.

James Saxton Sometime after his father-in-law built the Saxton House, James Saxton moved into the home at Market and Fourth. He was a prominent banker in Canton.

Photo of young Ida McKinley called "Her engagement picture", taken probably earlier c. 1867-68 As a young woman, Ida Saxton was well-educated, traveled through Europe and then worked her way up through several positions at her father's bank.

Profile of William McKinley Born in Niles, Ohio, William McKinley came to Canton as a young man, initially drawn there by the presence of his sister. In time, he would become its best-known citizen.

McKinleys hiking out west (Ida in center) As a young woman, Ida McKinley was bright, intelligent and full of life. She is seen here with her husband and several friends on hike during her honeymoon out west.

He attended the Inauguration, but never again saw his sister, the First Lady. In 1898, his spurned lover, the married Mrs. Anna George, shot him on a dark street near the Saxton House. Anna had even made her way to the Saxton House, demanding that items she claimed were hers be returned.

In contrast, the Barbers (Ida's sister Mary's family) often made lengthy stays at the White House. The eldest child, Smith College graduate Mary Barber, even spent part of the social season from November to April with her aunt Ida, assisting her as First Lady. In October 1898, Pina (Mary) had come to stay with the McKinleys, as she made arrangements to bring home her son John, who was in Garfield Hospital in the capital. John was hospitalized with typhoid fever he contracted in Puerto Rico, while fighting in the Spanish-American War. Thus, Pina and Ida were both in the White House when they received word from Canton that George had been shot dead. The President, First Lady, Pina and John Barber rushed to Canton for the funeral. To avoid bringing further attention to the scandal, the President left for a scheduled trip west and the First Lady went to Chicago to stay with her cousin.

It was probably while he was in Canton during the summer of 1899 that the President finally was able to make arrangements to buy the house they had rented during the 1896 campaign – his and Ida's home for the first five years of marriage. The President and First Lady began making plans to retire there. They spent three days together just focused on the renovation plans for the house; McKinley later remarked that those three days were perhaps the happiest of their life together and that it seemed to recapture some of the hope of their honeymoon.

McKinley was re-elected to his second term in 1900. He and Ida were back in Canton during the late summer of 1901, after a west coast tour and before leaving for the Pan-American Exposition in Buffalo in September. On this trip back home, they slept in their old house. Since it was still undergoing some renovations, however, they spent much of their time at the Saxton House, to visit and dine with the Barbers. After the President's assassination in Buffalo in September, and following his Washington funeral and Canton burial, the widowed First Lady returned to live in Canton at the McKinley home. Dependent in every way on the Barbers, who still lived in the Saxton House, Mrs. McKinley was frequently back there with them. She died in 1907.

Postcard of McKinley Market Street house As newlyweds, William and Ida McKinley were given this home several blocks north from the Saxton House as a gift from her father.

As a clinical psychologist in private practice for many years, the restoration and renovation of a Victorian house hardly seemed like a logical next step in my life – but I volunteered for the job immediately.

Mary Regula had called me just after I had retired. I knew her, but not very well. She told me what she had in mind: creating a library and education center on the history of First Ladies. The educational aspect immediately appealed to me. Born and raised in Canada, I particularly understood the value of patriotism, and developed a great interest in American history. I had also noticed an increasing lack of knowledge about our history, even among adults. The earlier that one could capture the imagination of young people, the greater the chance that they would retain its value in contemporary life. Using the lives of prominent figures in history to make a larger statement can often engage the interests of people more than just statistics and dates.

I didn't know a lot about First Ladies but, through the years of my practice, I had often found myself in great awe of women who managed to live their lives and pull themselves up in society, often without anyone's help except their own. I liked the idea of recognizing the First Ladies because I also knew that, in a marriage, rarely does a spouse fail to discuss issues with their partner. Most women have a tremendous impact on family decisions yet, as I saw in my work, their value was often dismissed, diminished or wholly unrecognized. Mary Regula's project sounded interesting. I accepted her invitation to be one of thirteen women to meet to help establish the library and work as a volunteer.

I have always been naturally drawn to the Victorian era, appreciating the old world look, even wearing high laced-up boots, and clothing inspired by the style of that time. I have also always loved architecture, particularly that which retained all of its craftsmanship, most frequently seen in Europe. I designed most of the interiors of my own homes through the years and embraced definitive, bright – but grayed down - color just as much as the Victorians did. As the meetings continued everyone took a different part. Since many people had been to my home, and seen the Victoriana I had there, several members suggested I take on the task of overseeing the restoration and renovation of the old Saxton House that we hoped to make our central office, library, education and research center.

As a full-time volunteer, It was quite a challenge. The first step was coming to understand the history of the family that had lived there and the context in which Ida Saxton McKinley matured. This involved a closer study of her upbringing, her personality, her husband, her health and her role as First Lady.

Postcard of Ida McKinley in her sitting room during 1896 campaign Ida McKinley suffered from numerous illnesses including epilepsy by the time her husband ran for president. Here she is seen in her sitting room during the 1896 campaign.

Ribbon and picture pin of Ida McKinley for Canton McKinley Women's Club Although women did not yet have the vote, campaign managers found that the story of William McKinley's devotion to Ida not only stopped wild rumors about her "real" condition, but appealed to male voters looking for moral purity in a candidate.

Ida McKinley ashtray (top), **Ida McKinley stereocard** (middle), **McKinley Romance book** (bottom) As both a candidate's wife and a President's wife, Ida McKinley was a sympathetic public figure. Her image was used on everything from ashtrays to the popular stereo-optical cards of the era. McKinley's devotion to her was even celebrated in verse, in a small book *A McKinley Romance*.

We knew that the house was built in two parts, the present-day back section in approximately 1840 and the front section in approximately 1870. To illustrate the residency period of both Ida Saxton and William McKinley, we decided to date the restored and renovated interior in the front portion of the house to the 1870s and 1880s. Considering the wealth inherited by the Saxton children after the death of their parents, we realized that the house would have had some of the finest appointments available at the time. Since the house was passed down in the family, some of the older furniture of the Saxtons would have been sentimentally retained, and mixed in with many newer and finer pieces. There would have been a great many varieties of style, from the early to the latter Victorian age.

Another factor that helped guide the direction of the project was examining the type of environment in which Ida McKinley lived. With her delicate health, we know that most of the hours of her adult life were spent indoors. The only times she would usually step outside were for a morning carriage ride or, with her husband, at an evening event. Her rooms were more than just places to eat, sleep and relax. Wherever she lived, her exacting standards and excellent tastes would be evident. We know of her personal tastes from the exquisitely rich tastes in her clothing. She purchased most of her clothes from Marshall Field's in Chicago because her cousin Mary Goodman McWilliams was married to a manager there, and she was given great discounts. Marshall Field's was among the most famous exclusive department stores in Gilded Age America. As her clothes and other items attest, there was nothing provincial in her style. Her early exposure to European, particularly Parisian, influences is evident. One could not imagine her living in an unfashionable setting, or with a lot of old furniture from her parents. With Governors, Ohio officials, United States Senators and McKinley's fellow Congressmen coming to visit, she certainly would have wanted the public rooms to be restrained showplaces. Finally, while the Barbers lived in the house full-time, they were devoted not only to Ida's well-being but also to McKinley's career, wanting to do all they could to help him. Despite the fact that the house was filled with children and three adults, they all made it McKinley's home when he was in town.

These were the basic facts we had when I began to plan the restoration and renovation of the house. With most of the rooms envisioned as being used as office and library space, we initially intended to only restore the front parlor. With this agenda, I began to do intensive research on what such a room – at that time, in this part of the country – would have looked like. I contacted the Victorian Society of America, and the National Trust for Historic Preservation for reference and suggestions. I bought dozens of books on Victorian furniture and interiors. I contacted merchants who dealt in historic hardware, lighting fixtures, carpeting, furniture and wallpaper that I had previously worked with in doing my own Victorian home projects.

Slowly we began to put pieces together, always questioning if it would have been in this kind of room by these kinds of people. Unfortunately, of the photographs that we do have of the Saxton House interiors, we do not have one of this main parlor. Being a Congressional wife, then Governor's wife, Ida McKinley would have made this a more formal parlor, a room where guests would be received, as opposed to the "private," family parlor. Everyone on the committee liked the idea of using the ashes of roses and green colors of the era that were typical. Also in typical style of the wealthy Victorians, a variety of contrasting wallpapers would be used. We ended up using twenty-three separate patterns. Everything fit in like a jigsaw puzzle. One of the original fireplaces was donated by descendants of the Saxton family and put back in its place in this parlor. We have not been able to yet return to the house all the Saxton and McKinley family items that are still available. The McKinley Museum, however, graciously loaned us several associated items of the families. We did get a portrait of Ida as a young woman from the Ohio Historical Association, and it now hangs in an oval frame above the fireplace. There is also a piano that belonged to Ida, a desk of the period and inkwell set with Ida's initials that are now on display here. Historic merchants helped fill in the gaps with appropriate furniture.

Where we have had a photo of a room, however, we have been able to copy its look. With a photograph, we have enlarged it – frequently time after time – until we could catch even a wisp of the detail from a framed photo, the curves on a carved piece of furniture, or the pattern of a rug. Ultimately, the Saxton-McKinley House represents both historic restoration and historic renovation. Restoration has involved finding an actual item that was in the house – even if it is not in the best condition - that would be carefully restored to its best possible condition and then placed back just where it was. Renovating has been a process of reconstructing a room back to its approximate look – even if that involves changing walls or doorframes – and choosing furniture and furnishings that give it the look of the era without actually being the original items that were in that room.

The entrance hall, for example, is based on the look of the era. William Morris, the designer whose work was very prolific during that period, felt very strongly that one should bring the outdoors inside. I found historic wallpaper that did just that – not a Victoriana floral print, but rather one with small flowers and leaves and some gilt in it. I found a chandelier for the entrance hall that is appropriate to the era. We were quite delighted when, some time later, in examining photographs of the Blue Room of the White House during the McKinley era, we noticed that our chandelier in that hall is similar to the one there, although ours is much smaller.

In contrast is William McKinley's office on the third floor. Luckily, we have a fairly clear photograph of this room as it looked while McKinley was a member of Congress and where he wrote the first protective tariff bill of 1890. On the one hand, we managed to figure out the framed images on the walls by blowing up the photograph of the room. On the other hand, the

Ida McKinley dress collar from Inaugural dress (top) **Picture of Ida McKinley in her Inaugural dress showing collar** (bottom) Ida McKinley had a rich taste in clothing, influenced by European styles. She is pictured here in her first Inaugural gown, the original dress collar for it now is in the National First Ladies' Library collection.

PRESIDENT'S RECEPTION TO THE DIPLOMATIC CORPS.

FIRST STATE FUNCTION AT WHITE HOUSE.

Ida McKinley receiving in chair with President at Diplomatic Corps reception As First Lady, Ida McKinley refused to permit her physical weaknesses handicap her assumption of the role of hostess. She insisted on receiving by the President's side at receptions, although she was seated in a large chair. In this newspaper illustration, she is portrayed as greeting the Diplomatic Corps.

Ida McKinley slippers (bottom right), **Picture of Ida McKinley knitting slippers** (bottom left) Ida McKinley did not adopt one particular "project" as many of her successors did, but she did create a unique form of supporting charities. An expert with the knitting needles and crochet hook, she made thousands of pairs of slippers and donated them to the numerous charities that requested the First Lady to send an item they could sell or auction for fundraising.

photo is just too dark to exactly reproduce the wallpaper; not enough of it is visible to get the full pattern. We sent the photo to various experts, and ultimately learned that it was a scenery style known as "Japonesque," a Victorian style influenced by Japanese motifs. Thus we went with something that was similar in size and in a "Japonesque" print. In the photo one can also make out that on the ceiling there is a wallpaper border of roses. We used something very similar. Many people are surprised at the sight of this – but it is there in the original photo. There are also a lot of bookcases in the photo, this being the congressman's study and office. We had local Amish woodworkers – Shrock's of Walnut Creek, who are renowned for their precise craft - build bookcases as exact copies, following the carvings of the originals. They were so excited about the project that they donated the finished bookcases. As for the roll-top desk in the photo, which McKinley used while he was congressman, we luckily found one that is similar. Finally, we have displayed a large version of the photo of the room so visitors can see exactly what it looked like.

A postcard of Mrs. McKinley, seated in a rocking chair in a sitting room, also showed that it was connected to her bedroom. We worked from the postcard, again blowing up different sections of it to catch the details – the carpet, what was on the table, the fireplace, etc. It led us, for example, to seek a little decorative oval black iron door that fit in the fireplace – which I found at a flea market. I contacted the historic merchants about the wallpaper, which I could make out in the postcard. Nobody could identify it. We checked also with the Cooper-Hewitt Museum experts on textiles and wallpaper, but they had no information on it. Finally, I contacted three firms that reproduce historic wallpaper. All three wanted to do it; only one, Scalamandre, could deliver it in the limited time before the house was

opened to the public. Scalamandre is the famous fabric and wallpaper house which also provided Jacqueline Kennedy with the silk wall coverings in the restored state rooms of the White House. They reproduced the wallpaper from scratch – beginning with the hand-drawing of the designs in it. Since the picture was black-and-white, we did not have the colors. We do know that Mrs. McKinley did not like yellow, but she did seem to favor blues and rose hues, and we went with that. In the postcard, we could see through the doorway of her bedroom that the walls had the same paper, so there were two rooms that had to be done with this paper. The wallpaper arrived on a Friday afternoon; the female wallpaper hanger hung it all in time for the Monday opening.

We knew from a photograph of the McKinley's White House bedroom that the couple brought their brass twin beds from Ohio, which were returned to Canton after the assassination. They are now housed in the

McKinleys walking on 1901 trip In the summer of 1901, the McKinleys were back in Canton. From there, they went to the Buffalo Exposition. Mrs. McKinley had just recently recovered from a near-fatal infection. Sadly, it was on this trip that the President was assassinated.

McKinley Museum. I spoke to antique dealers and showed them the photo. One finally called me: "I just came back from a huge antique show and brought a bed you are going to love. It is as close as possible to the one in the picture." It was quite close. Then I asked a board member to run out and start scouring around to find an appropriate bedspread, even if it were just temporary for the opening, which was in several days. She came back with two sample pieces of antique fabric. We were surprised that one of them was quite similar to Mrs. McKinley's bedspread, but we were shocked to discover that the fabric was made by Waverly and used for a Congressional wives luncheon for Rosalynn Carter, entitled "Roses for Rosalynn."

The process is continuing. We recently began restoring half of the first floor that was used for offices by a foundation until a few months ago. We plan to create a family parlor, a library alcove, a dining room, a breakfast room and a kitchen. We have a sketch of the original layout, hand drawn by

a elderly descendant of the Barbers, from her memories of being in the house as a young girl. We have some limitations, such as the elevator and back staircase, which were added in the early 1990s and which cut into this space, but we plan to locate these rooms as closely as possible to the floor plan sketch.

Another photo recently shown to us by descendants of the Barber family is of the family parlor. We had never seen it before. Prominent in the picture is a very unusual light fixture, with fringe on the shade and metal rolls at the top. While I was in Florida, we were parked near an odd, little lampshade store. Low and behold, there was the light fixture in it. As we were looking at it, the store owner remarked, 'Oh, that came from Cleveland, Ohio." It didn't have fringe

Barber children (top), **Ida McKinley with Pina Barber's grand-children** (bottom) Ida McKinley returned to live out the last six years of her life in Canton. Although she lived in the old house where she and McKinley had first begun their married life, she was often with the family of her sister Pina Barber in the Saxton House. The seven Barber children, a group of them seen here, were devoted to her. The photo of several of Pina Barber's grandchildren with the former First Lady is perhaps one of the last taken of her.

on it, but it had little holes at the bottom of the shade where the fringe would have been - and metal rolls at the top. That night I phoned the store and let it ring until an answering machine came on: "Don't sell that lamp, I'm buying it as soon as your store opens", I said. Since there is no specific provenance on the piece, we cannot say definitively that it is the one used by the Barbers and the McKinleys, though it certainly does seem to be. I am seeking to trace back the lamp's exact origins from this region of Ohio.

The dining room will also be done, and we will start that process by working outward from the wallpaper. Not long ago, I received a phone call from the wallpaper division of the Cooper-Hewitt Museum. They had received a letter from a museum in Spain, which had in its collection wallpaper that was "made expressedly for Mrs. McKinley" and used in the White House. It was labeled Forget Me Not Blue. They had sent the Cooper-Hewitt Museum a snapshot of the paper, which was blue and gold, but the flash had diluted the color. The museum sent us the snapshot, and we immediately telephoned the Spanish museum for further information. Although the staff person who had originally sent the picture was no longer an employee she happened to be there at that moment for a meeting. She didn't think the museum would either loan the paper for us to copy or cut a small piece for us to have reproduced. "But," she said in an afterthought, "if you really have a problem, I have a little piece of it myself and can send it along." I called Scalamandre, and they said they would copy it. We later found a White House photo of Ida in her second inaugural ball gown with this wallpaper showing in the background.

There are so many Saxton, Barber and McKinley family objects and items we hope to retrieve or that will find their way back to the house. We will continue to actively seek these items.

These are just some of the trails and clues one must follow in the process of restoring an historic site like the Saxton-McKinley House. From a private home held by four generations of a prominent Canton family, to a saloon, to a boarding house where rooms were rented by the hour, the evolution of the house is a tale within itself. Pina Barber's grandson, Marsh Belden, Sr. finally bought the deteriorating building in 1978 when he learned that a wrecking ball was poised to destroy his family's old home. Through the generosity of his family, the nation now has not only the only remaining home of the 25th President of the United States and his First Lady, but also a site honoring all of her predecessors and successors.

[1] See Colonel W. H. Crook, *Memories of the White House: Personal Recollections of Colonel W. H. Crook* (Boston: Little, Brown, 1911) P. 260 and *The Christian Advocate*, June 22, 1903

19th century photo of the family parlor Work on the rooms of the Saxton-McKinley House is continuing. A recently discovered photo of the family parlor, for example, is guiding the recreation of that room.

Restored ballroom on third floor with photo of Dr. Sheila Fisher (author of this chapter)

The restored formal parlor (top left), **The restored McKinley office** (middle left), **The restored sitting room of Ida McKinley** (bottom right), **The restored bedroom of Ida McKinley** (top right), **Ida McKinley's piano on display in the formal Parlor** (middle right) The rooms of the Saxton-McKinley House have been carefully returned to the way they may have once looked based on historical documentation, period styles, and old photographs.

THE EDUCATION AND RESEARCH CENTER

By Patricia A. Krider, Executive Director of the National First Ladies' Library

There's no magic like the magic of the written word.

-Laura Bush

Amazingly, there was no permanent library in the White House until a full half-century after the building was first occupied. Presidents had simply brought their books with them and, when the term was finished, simply returned home with them. It took a former schoolteacher to put an end to this.

Abigail Powers Fillmore, the first First Lady to earn her own living, worked as a teacher in Sempronius, in Cayuga County, New York, before and after her 1826 marriage – to one of her students, carpenter Millard Fillmore. She taught him to write and speak correctly, and study geography with a map. Coming out of poverty she highly prized the value of education. She was taught to read by her mother from her late father's collection of books. Wanting other working-class families to have the same opportunity for self-improvement, she started the first public circulation library in town by selling two-dollar subscriptions. After the Fillmores moved to Buffalo, and then to nearby East Aurora in the far northwestern portion of the state, she began assembling an impressive library of over 4,000 volumes in their

Abigail Fillmore photo (top), **Drawing of 19th century oval room White House library** (bottom middle), **Mary Abigail Fillmore playing harp** (bottom right) The first First Lady to come from the working class and to support herself in a full-time job, Abigail Fillmore was a schoolteacher who highly valued education. She created the first permanent White House library in 1850. Here the Fillmores gathered to read and relax, often entertained by their daughter Mary Abigail Fillmore who played her harp, and also assisted her mother on social occasions. Located in the oval room of the family quarters, special rounded bookcases were built to hold the books. This engraving shows the room some fifteen years later, under the Andrew Johnson Administration.

homes. In middle age, Abigail even taught herself French, took piano lessons and reported to her husband in one letter, "Have finished studying the maps of ancient geography." One observer noted that, "Mrs. Fillmore was a woman who had read much and was well-informed on all the topics of the day, and Mr. Fillmore had the highest respect for her attainments, and has been heard to say he never took any important step without her counsel and advice." [1]

Within a month of moving into the White House in October 1850 (Fillmore had been Vice President and became President that July upon the death of President Zachary Taylor), Abigail Fillmore was refurbishing the oval parlor in the family quarters, on the second floor (which one walks through today to get to the Truman Balcony). Although Abigail's piano and her daughter Mary Abigail's harp were placed there, it would not be a music room, but a library. Curved bookcases were especially built, and the First Lady persuaded her husband to successfully seek a Congressional appropriation for several hundred leather-bound volumes. Mrs. Fillmore got a two thousand dollars appropriation from Congress and began choosing the volumes that would create the first White House library. The complete works of Shakespeare, studies of world religions, American law, some contemporary romantic novels, histories of most parts of the world, the biographies of legendary figures of American history, travelogues, and the works of popular Scottish poet Robert Burns composed the collection.

Just over a century later, another First Lady took up the cause begun by Abigail Fillmore. In the interim years, the original Fillmore library collection

Cartoon of Kennedy family reading books (middle), **Jackie Kennedy and her restoration committee gathered for group photo** (bottom) Since the books of Abigail Fillmore's White House library disappeared over the years, Jacqueline Kennedy created the second permanent White House library on the ground floor as part of the overall restoration plans of her preservation committee, with whom she meets here in the Red Room. Seated beside her is James Babb of the Yale University library who served as head of the acquisitions committee for the library. Jackie Kennedy's own intense interest in literature and history was shared by the President and encouraged even in their little daughter Caroline – a point humorously made in this vintage cartoon of the family.

Photograph of front of new National First Ladies' Library Education and Research Center The former City National Bank of Canton has been painstakingly renovated into a Victorian library – yet with state-of-the-art 21st century technology. It is just one block north of the Saxton-McKinley House.

Two Renderings of the Education and Research Center Library Floor The National First Ladies' Library Education and Research Center provides ample space for researchers. In addition to the stacks, there are study carrels, meeting rooms and a theater for educational presentations.

dissipated – books became worn and were probably sold at the numerous auctions of "unusable" historic items that many presidents held. Although they were, in fact, government property and purchased with the intention of remaining as permanent White House objects, some of the books were borrowed and not returned, and certainly taken either by staff or members of presidential families. There was no curator or other household staff member charged with maintaining the library.

Then, in 1961, as part of her overall restoration of the White House rooms, Jacqueline Kennedy sought to create the permanent White House library in a ground floor room. Asking presidential advisor, the distinguished historian and author Arthur M. Schlesinger, Jr., to assist her, Mrs. Kennedy named James Babb of the Yale University library to head her acquisitions committee. There was space for only fifteen hundred volumes, and Mrs. Kennedy wanted it to "contain the most significant works of American history and literature and that the list should be made public." [2] Titles were carefully chosen to reflect general American history and presidential history. Although she did not want the White House staff to rush the small room and then have the books "all start disappearing," she also believed that "a library is dead if not used." [3] Scholarly biographies of all the presidents were included in Mrs. Kennedy's collection.

It was with a similar sense of mission, of creating a permanent center of specialized knowledge and study, that the National First Ladies' Library was born. Outgrowing the original site, the Saxton-McKinley House, the library began to cast about for another nearby and appropriate site to create a large state-of-the-art facility where students and historians alike could come to study, research and learn. Meanwhile, dozens and dozens of donated and acquired books on or related to First Ladies, drawn from the lists of its comprehensive bibliography, were gathering in nooks and closets and offices in the Saxton-McKinley house. Yet again, as they had done with the house, the collateral descendants of Ida Saxton McKinley came through. In 1998, a century after their great-great-aunt Ida served as First Lady, the Marsh Belden, Sr. family donated the City National Bank Building to the National First Ladies' Library. Built in 1895 – while William and Ida McKinley were just living down the street – the City

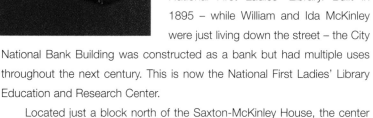

National Bank Building was constructed as a bank but had multiple uses throughout the next century. This is now the National First Ladies' Library Education and Research Center.

Located just a block north of the Saxton-McKinley House, the center has seven floors with approximately 20,000 square feet of usable space. Its large skylight over the main banking room on the first floor has been fully restored, as has a portion of the translucent glass block floor just beneath the skylight. The upper floors of the building are designed in a "U" shape with two wings connected by a lobby that create a "light well" for the skylight below. On the first floor foyer and lobby, main reception/exhibit room and lobbies of the upper floors there is beautiful, polished, Tennessee pink marble. Transom windows were used throughout the building to bring additional light into the rooms.

Where once there had been various commercial shops – including a barbershop and public baths on the lower level there will now be a magnificent 91-seat Victorian Theater. Outside the theater, the lobby resembles a street scene with brick walkway and storefront displays. Entering the theater through antique brass doors, visitors come to take in films, documentaries, author lectures, symposiums, first-person performances and other educational presentations. There is also an authentic Victorian Reproduco located here, an automated musical instrument that can produce both piano and organ music through the use of rolls.

The first floor has a large reception room that also serves as a meeting room and exhibition space. Also located in this room is the restored skylight and glass block floor. A small library room is located at the rear of the first floor. A spiral stairwell in this library leads to a mezzanine where especially fragile, rare and valuable books are held. The massive, monumental staircase of cast iron railings, a carved wood handrail and slate steps – inscribed with donor names – leads to the upper floors.

Climbing the stairs to the second floor, researchers and visitors now come to the main library, with shelving and reading room. There is an east library and west library with ample research and study space connected by a lobby with marble floors and wainscoting. Nearly all of the old office walls have been removed here, but the original transom windows are still in place, indicating where the walls were once located.

Seminars, workshops and other meetings are held in a large conference room on the third floor. Nearby are smaller, private rooms for researchers. On the fourth floor, library staff maintains its offices. Archival material and other original manuscripts and papers are held in temperature-controlled, secure rooms on the upper two floors, along with spaces for offices, classrooms and other smaller conference rooms.

Extensive renovation and upgrading made the building adaptable for twenty-first century needs like computers, database and photo-duplication machines, film, and audiotape and videotape players. Yet under the direction of Dr. Sheila Fisher, the general contractor carefully preserved and installed original Victorian or period-simulated lighting fixtures. Custom-designed library furniture, which was made in Massachusetts, Colorado and Ohio, incorporates some of the architectural details of the building such as the egg and dart pattern found in crown molding and the fleur de lis and rosette found on the monumental staircase. The painstakingly comprehen-

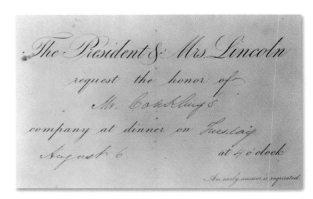

Book of reproduction Mary Lincoln letters in the Illinois archives (top and middle), **Book of Jane Pierce Letters** (bottom) Among the thousands of book titles to be found in the library are many of the published volumes of First Lady correspondence, including a volume of Mary Lincoln's, a gift from Illinois Governor's wife, and one of Jane Pierce's letters, privately printed by a collector of her letters to her sister Mary Aiken and her family.

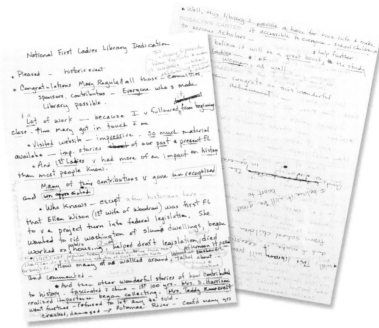

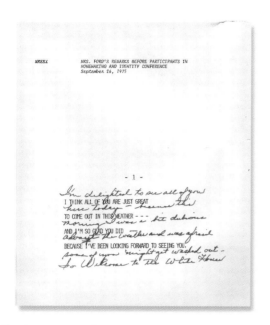

Betty Ford's speech (top left), **Notes from Rosalynn Carter speech from dedication of National First Ladies' Library** (top right), **Florence Harding diary** (middle left), **Rosalynn Carter's Congressional testimony text** (middle right), **Cover of pamphlet "First Lady Conference on Drug Abuse at United Nations"** (bottom right) Original manuscript materials pertaining to First Ladies are already part of the National First Ladies' Library's collection and are also being actively sought. A variety of some examples include the speech of Betty Ford to a homemaker's group, with the First Lady's handwritten notes and corrections on it, notes from Rosalynn Carter's speech at the opening of the National First Ladies' Library, Rosalynn Carter's testimony before Congress, Nancy Reagan's first address to the United Nations, and an amazing calendar book which Florence Harding used as a diary of sorts, recording her most intimate thoughts.

The
First Ladies
Conference
on
Drug Abuse

At the United Nations
October 21, 1985

sive process was at a cost of some $6 million.

Each of the seven floors is named for the First Ladies born or who lived in Ohio, or whose husbands were Ohioans when elected President: Anna (Mrs. William Henry) Harrison, Lucy (Mrs. Rutherford B.) Hayes, Lucretia (Mrs. James A.) Garfield, Caroline (Mrs. Benjamin Harrison, Ida (Mrs. William) McKinley, Nellie (Mrs. William Howard) Taft, and Florence (Mrs. Warren G.) Harding.

The National First Ladies' Library Education and Research Center not only houses the only definitive collection of books, pamphlets and other printed materials related to the First Ladies for the use of students and historians alike, but also the research materials, papers and manuscripts of published biographies of First Ladies such as Florence Harding, Nellie Taft and Jacqueline Kennedy. The Library is continuing to seek the papers of First Lady and presidential biographers and historians, journalists and others associated with First Lady history for its archives as the only National Historic Site devoted solely to the topic. While it will not attempt to reproduce the entire collections of First Ladies papers that already exist as part of the archives of individual presidential libraries, it does seek original letters, diaries and other manuscript materials written by First Ladies which shed light on the individual women's lives and also illuminate the evolving role of First Lady in the American history and culture. Photocopies and original out-of-print newspaper and magazine articles, as well as important manuscripts of First Ladies are also actively being sought for the archives.

Photo of magazines and press reaction to Hillary Clinton for heading Health Care Reform Thousands of newspaper and magazine articles about First Ladies are a major part of the National First Ladies' Library holdings, including the many written about Hillary Clinton's multiple roles.

THE INAUGURATION OF PRESIDENT CLEVELAND, MARCH 4TH.—THE PRESIDENT, WITH HIS SISTERS, RECEIVING GUESTS IN HIS ROOM ADJOINING THE BALLROOM.
FROM A SKETCH BY C. UPHAM.—SEE PAGE 54.

Rose Elizabeth Cleveland receiving at Inaugural Ball with her brother Rose Elizabeth Cleveland who served as her brother's First Lady before his 1886 marriage, wrote novels, poetry and other books which became best sellers.

Permanent and temporary exhibits are displayed for the visiting public at the center. First Ladies' personal possessions, handwritten letters and photographs are among the items that are and will continue to be displayed. In addition, items of First Ladies' clothing will be exhibited. Showing such items of clothing, however, will not only reflect how First Ladies sought to create their public images, but will also illustrate the progress of technology in fabric manufacturing and evolving popular tastes over time. Exhibits focus not only on the lives and accomplishments of individual First Ladies but also explore aspects of women's history, political issues, social influences and other topics and themes related to the role of First Lady. The center's staff is continuing to collect and seek all forms of objects and items reflecting the library's mission.

As part of its ongoing educational efforts, the center's theater serves as a gathering place for regional and national school groups, grades K to 12, who have participated in curriculum units on First Ladies developed with the library. Other programs, such as film festival weeks that will show dramatic portrayals of White House life, presidential and First Lady biographical depictions, are anticipated for the theater as well. A comfortable and elegant venue for stage presentations focusing on the First Ladies and related women's, presidential and general history, the theater is also the site of lively lectures, debates, panel discussions and other educational presentations. The Library will host regularly scheduled symposia focused on a specific First Lady or related subject, bringing together distinguished historians, biographers, former White House staff members and other experts, prompting a deeper understanding not only of the individual First Ladies but the context of the times they lived and the issues which involved them.

The coincidental fact that the only First Lady who has a graduate degree in library sciences and worked as a librarian is in the White House at the time of the opening of the National First Ladies' Library Education and Research Center seems highly appropriate. Laura Bush has long loved the world of books and appreciated the value of public libraries. In the same year that the center opened, 2003, her own dedication to the concept of the public library, and influence with the President on the matter, emerged quite publicly when she announced that her husband's 2004 federal spending request in the national budget asked Congress for a 15 percent increase in federal funds of libraries and museums over the previous year, with the prospect of dispensing some $242 million for the Institute of Museum and Library Services, which dispenses federal dollars to the nation's 122,000 libraries and 15,000 museums. Also, for 2003, the First Lady declared that the President proposed creating a $10 million fund dedicated to addressing the nation's shortage of librarians, 58 percent of whom are projected to retire by 2019. For 2004, she said, there was a request for $20 million for that program.

Robert Martin, the Institute's director, remarked, "In preparing to make the first grants for this initiative, we heard compelling stories about the need for librarians and a wealth of ideas for creative solutions. The library community is grateful to the President and Mrs. Bush for their commitment to learning and to libraries." [4]

[1] Bess Furman Papers, Container 75, file folder #1, Library of Congress, Manuscript Division

[2] Jacqueline Kennedy Onassis to Carl Anthony, December 3, 1987 and December 8, 1989, quoted in Anthony, *First Ladies*, volume 2, p. 33

[3] see letters of Jacqueline Kennedy to Arthur M. Schlesinger, Jr. on the White House library, July 24, 1961, February 21, 1963 and April 3, 1963, all Box W-7, Schlesinger Papers, John F. Kennedy Presidential Library

[4] "Bush Eyes Fed Budget Hike for Libraries," Associated Press story, January 23, 2003 and "Budget Boost Overdue, Nation's Libraries Say," by Linton Weeks, *The Washington Post*, January 28, 2003

Edith Roosevelt at her desk in hallway of family quarters
(Opposite page) Edith Roosevelt enjoyed doing her own historical research and honed the craft of writing, turning out writings – both published and unpublished – on her global travels and Connecticut history.

PERSONAL POSSESSIONS AND OBJECTS OF FIRST LADIES IN THE NATIONAL FIRST LADIES' LIBRARY COLLECTION

A. Florence Harding's black silk dress & fur coat (top left)
B. Florence Harding's hat (middle left)
C. Florence Harding's black silk dress (bottom left)
D. Lady Bird Johnson's gloves (middle)
E. Lady Bird Johnson with white gloves (bottom right)

F. Lucy Hayes in white dress (top left)
G. Lucy Hayes' white dress (bottom left)
H. Fan painted by Caroline Harrison (top right)
I. Caroline Harrison holding fan (bottom right)

J. Nancy Reagan wearing Adolfo hat (top left)

K. Nancy Reagan's Adolfo hat (bottom left)

L. Rosalynn Carter's evening gown (top right)

M. Rosalynn Carter in red evening gown (bottom right)

N. Lucretia Garfield in bonnet (top left)
O. Lucretia Garfield's bonnet (bottom left)

P. Mary Johnson Stover's cap (top right)
Q. Mary Johnson Stover (bottom right)

Photo courtesy of the National Park Service, Andrew Johnson National Historical Society

A - Q (page 50-53) Among the holdings of the National First Ladies' Library that are rotated for display on the ground floor and first floor exhibition areas are clothing and other personal objects owned and used by First Ladies. They reveal not only how a First Lady chose to craft her public image but also the evolution of fashions that reflect technological, socioeconomic and cultural elements. Among the items and pictures illustrating them are: Florence Harding's hat and dress worn on the ill-fated 1923 Alaskan trip during which her husband died; a roller-brimmed hat worn by Nancy Reagan in the Sixties, when her husband was Governor of California; "opera" white gloves worn by Lady Bird Johnson for formal White House events; a white gown worn by Lucy Hayes and a picture showing her in a similar one; a fan hand-painted and used by First Lady Caroline Harrison and her Inaugural gown picture in which she carries a fan; a bonnet worn by Lucretia Garfield, pictured wearing a similar one; a cherry-red evening gown worn by Rosalynn Carter at a state dinner; the simple lace cap of Mary Johnson Stover who aided her sister Martha Patterson, in her duties as White House hostess while filling in for her ill mother, Eliza Johnson.

JACKIE KENNEDY 1929-1994

REPUBLIQUE DU TCHAD

Rosalynn Carter silver commemorative coin (top left), **Helen Taft gold commemorative coin** (middle left), **Martha Washington silver certificate** (top right), **Jackie Kennedy Onassis government stamps from Republique of Tchad** (bottom left) The use of the images of First Ladies as commemoratives on everything from coin collections to the cash and postage stamps are also collected by the National First Ladies' Library: a silver coin of Rosalynn Carter, a gold coin of Nellie Taft, a U.S. government's silver certificate dollar from 1891 depicting Martha Washington and postage stamps honoring Jacqueline Kennedy Onassis from the Republique of Tchad are just a sample.

Original sketch of Ellen Wilson (top left), **Martha Washington oil portrait** (top right) The collection of original artwork and imagery of the First Ladies is also part of the center's holdings, including this preliminary portrait handsketch of Ellen Wilson, and a 19th century portrait of Martha Washington, adapted from the familiar life portrait by Gilbert Stuart.

Hillary Clinton at announcement of National First Ladies' Library as Save America's Treasure project (above) Seen here on July 23, 1999, First Lady Hillary Clinton came to Canton to announce that the renovation of the City National Bank into the National First Ladies' Library Education and Research Center had been chosen as one of the Official Projects of the Save America's Treasures program she began.

Laura Bush reading in library to children (above) Laura Bush, a former schoolteacher and librarian has focused her effort on early childhood development, education reform and federal assistance to public libraries.

PHOTOGRAPHING THE FIRST LADIES

The National First Ladies' Library Audio-Visual Collection by Craig Schermer, Historian

Oh, now you're not here to photograph us, are you…?

Jacqueline Kennedy

"Lady Washington" oval print Although it bore no resemblance whatsoever to the real Martha Washington, this rudimentary engraving, printed in large quantities for sale to Americans of the post-Revolutionary Era, suggests that there was a public interest early in what the wife of the first President looked like.

Pursuing a passion for history can end up creating a bit of history itself sometimes. Like Mary Regula, my own interest in First Ladies was sparked by the same figure of tragedy, intelligence and controversy – Mrs. Abraham Lincoln. I was only eight years old when my father, a reservist stationed at Fort Leavenworth, first brought me to Springfield, Illinois to see the home of the Lincolns. Leaving with some sort of pamphlet or flyer, I found myself staring at the profile of Mary Lincoln on the cover, wondering just who this woman was. I knew about Abraham Lincoln, but never gave her any thought. Soon enough I was at the library, pouring through Ruth Painter Randall's newly published biography of Mrs. Mary Lincoln, *Biography of a Marriage*. I read it in two days. In 1959, while prowling an antique store with my parents, I came across a small cardboard card with a faded but familiar figure – Mrs. Lincoln. Thirty dollars was a lot of money for an eleven-year old then, but I saved and saved – and bought my first photograph of a First Lady. Little did I know how it would guide my life.

About ten years later, the respected artist and Lincoln portrait scholar Lloyd Ostendorf published *The Photographs of Mary Todd Lincoln*, which contained all the known pictures of her. He came to Cleveland to lecture on Abraham Lincoln but I brought my copy of his book on Mrs. Lincoln for him to autograph. Ostendorf was a kind and encouraging mentor of sorts, certainly a guide. There were 26 known photographs of Mrs. Lincoln. I made it my goal to obtain a copy of each one of them. I began hunting them down. I sought copies from historical societies, found other carte de visite and engravings at auctions and flea markets. Ostendorf himself gave me several copies of pictures he had. Imagine his surprise then, when I discovered in the Western Reserve Historical Society an unknown photograph of Mrs. Lincoln – not in the Ostendorf book!

I began to collect any books that had different photographs, portraits, drawings and sketches of Mrs. Lincoln – and naturally that usually meant collective biographies of First Ladies. Soon enough I found myself again intensely, strongly drawn to the faces of three others – all from Ohio – Caroline Harrison, Ida McKinley and Lucy Hayes. Much of their character and hardships seemed to be etched in the untouched pictures of them. I had also begun to do oil portraits by this time. One of the goals I had was to eventually paint a series of canvases which grouped together about five to eight First Ladies on each canvas, and do them all, from Washington to Nixon. That started me on the road to collecting pictures of them, but I was drawn to trying to find unusual pictures. I grew tired of seeing the same ones over and over. To this day, books that come out on First Ladies still use the familiar, stock – and frankly, rather lifeless – pictures. And too, numerous books still occasionally incorrectly identify them, switching one for another without much concern for accuracy. I wanted to rectify this. Realizing I would never be able to afford the high costs of collecting three-dimensional objects or original manuscripts of First Ladies, I thought that collecting photographs of them would be a more realistic way of building a private collection related to them. Capturing their personalities, their activities – their character – set me on as much of an historical adventure as trying to hunt down a manuscript or letter.

The first thing I had to do was to learn how to use a camera. It took me about a year to save enough to buy a really good second-hand camera. A great friend, Linda Sammon, taught me how to use it. I learned "on-the-job" so to speak during my first trip to the Library of Congress Prints and Photographs presidential collection, in 1984. By then I had become quite fascinated with Florence Harding – another Ohio First Lady. So Linda and I began by photographing original pictures of her, including the vast Herbert E. French collection, pictures taken by a press photographer who covered the White House from Taft through Coolidge. By the end of that first day, we must have taken about thirty rolls of film – all just on Mrs. Harding. By doing so, it lent another, more intensely real and personal understanding of an individual forgotten by or caricatured by history; this sparked my desire to do that with the others.

The second time I went to the Library of Congress, a year later, I went by myself and began systematically going through each one in chronological order, making copies of every picture that sparked my interest or said something unusual about the individuals – first portraits, then full-length, and then images showing a First Lady involved in some activity, where she was the center of attention. This further expanded my understanding of the evolution of the First Lady's role. That's when I began to run into prints and portraits and cartoons of the First Ladies as well. For me, the term "First Lady" also encompasses those daughters, sisters, nieces and other relatives who

Partially-completed Martha Washington portrait by Gilbert Stuart (top), **Partially-completed Abigail Adams portrait by Gilbert Stuart** (bottom) Gilbert Stuart was an unofficial sort of "court portraitist" to the first two Federalist presidential families and the political elite of the era. He left his paintings done from live sittings of both Martha Washington and Abigail Adams unfinished once he captured their facial characteristics. He made a tidy fortune by permitting other painters and engravers to use their faces and then adapt them to period clothing.

served as White House hostesses. I still have many unaccomplished, albeit esoteric intentions such as finally tracking down some image – picture, portrait or engraving – of Abby Kent Means, the friend and aunt-by-marriage to Jane Pierce, who fairly held together that bereaved family.

In my research on the pictures, my eyes became especially drawn to the detail that was apparent in the original glass plate negatives. For example, the sheen of the taffeta in Mary Lincoln's gown is lost in the reproductions made from it, particularly in that first carte de visite I had bought when I was young; every time you take a copy of a picture you lose upwards of twenty percent of the detail. Out of all of this grew a determination to find as many original images as I could – in whatever form they were available. With this goal in mind, I began to uncover numerous gems such as previously unpublished pictures of Mary Arthur McElroy and Caroline Harrison, and snapshot candids of Nancy Reagan and Hillary Clinton.

From the very beginning of the presidency, there was an interest in capturing and conveying the visual image of First Ladies. Even though it had no resemblance to its subject, an engraving of Martha Washington made for widespread reproduction and sale depicted her with the title "Lady Washington" surrounding the oval. Dolley Madison was the first First Lady to be accurately pictured for the American people when she was featured on the cover of Port Folio magazine, printed in Philadelphia, in its April 1818 issue (thirteen months after she left the White House). The engraving was copied from her portrait by Ezra Ames, now in the New York Historical Society collection. This technique was the only manner in which the visage

Julia Tyler – first First Lady to be photographed (top), Julia Gardiner Tyler was the first First Lady to be photographed, in 1844.

Color lithograph of Sarah Polk (right), Frequently written about because she employed her personal and strict religious beliefs to govern entertaining in the White House, Sarah Polk was a subject of considerable public interest. The first color lithograph portraying her was produced and sold to the public.

of prominent Americans, like Presidents and military leaders, could be seen by citizens in the early 19th century, By 1841, some enterprising engraver had managed to locate and receive permission from eight former presidential families to copy portraits of First Ladies Martha Washington to Angelica Van Buren. By 1845, lithography had progressed far enough to afford citizens color-tinted portraits of celebrities such as its First Lady, Sarah Polk.

The first incumbent First Lady to be photographed was Julia Tyler. Taken by the Anthony studios in New York the year of her marriage, 1844, the original daguerreotype is now in the collections of the Library of Congress. Mrs. Tyler may have posed for the picture with President Tyler in the studio either just before or after their surprise marriage on June 26, 1844 at the Church of the Ascension in that city. It is unlikely, however, that the picture was taken with the intention of it being copied and widely distributed to the public since no prints or engravings were based on it. Instead, that same year, her portrait by Francesco Anelli was copied and sold on a print, with the caption "The President's Bride."

Shortly thereafter in Washington, former First Lady Dolley Madison posed for several daguerreotypes, making her the earliest First Lady to be captured by the camera. One of the more interesting pictures she posed for was with a group of several prominent figures, including the President and

Mary Lincoln carte de visite picture (top), **Original glass plate negative of Mary Lincoln** (bottom) The first decades of portrait photography were done as image transfers onto glass. Seen here is the original glass negative of Mary Lincoln, showing the worry and tension of her character. In the 1850s, technology permitted the cheaper and massive reproduction of paper copies of the original, but the details were diluted by the transfer, as a carte de visite of the same image illustrates.

No. 204—Vol. XI.]   NEW YORK, DECEMBER 15, 1860.   [Price 6 Cts.

MRS. ABRAHAM LINCOLN, WIFE OF THE PRESIDENT ELECT, AND SONS.—FROM A PHOTOGRAPH BY F. DUYES, OF SPRINGFIELD, ILL.—SEE PAGE 30.

Mary Lincoln and two sons (top), **Mary Lincoln and family** (bottom), During the Civil War, there was considerably more newspaper coverage of the First Lady. Mary Lincoln's image was frequently portrayed. Technology did not yet permit for the printing of actual photographs in newspapers and magazines. Thus, existing photographs of her and her family were pasted onto an entirely fictional domestic scene, as the print below shows, or newspaper sketch artists copied actual photographs by drawing the images in ink pen or pencil by hand, as the 1861 newspaper image of Mrs. Lincoln and her sons Tad and Willie shows.

Mrs. Polk, and future President and First Lady James Buchanan and his niece Harriet Lane. In a beautiful joint photograph, the President and Mrs. Polk posed arm-in-arm. No presidential couple would so formally pose until the Hayeses in the 1870s, although a picture was snapped of General Grant at his Civil War headquarters, showing his wife in the doorway behind him.

Technology by the 1850s permitted the mass reproduction of daguerreotypes from their glass plate form to paper. Thus, the small card-sized carte de visite picture came into vogue. Not only were American families now able to pose for a picture and send copies to their relatives, but the likes of famous citizens could be purchased, collected and tucked into photographic albums which had empty paper frames on each page. The first First Lady whose picture was sold in this manner, through the studio of Matthew Brady – which owned the original glass negative – was Abigail Fillmore, and it was apparently a popular seller. Several such pictures were taken and sold of Mary Todd Lincoln in this manner during her four years as First Lady and she became the first First Lady whose accurate visual image was well known throughout the nation. Mrs. Lincoln, realizing that her very image was the real matter at hand, seized the opportunity to shape her public impression; her pictures were not to be copied and distributed by Brady unless she had given her prior approval of the image in question. Mrs. Lincoln herself was interested in pictures of First Ladies: in her Springfield, Illinois home, she had an oval engraving of Martha Washington.

As First Ladies became accustomed to literally becoming public property, they too shaped their image. Julia Grant, sensitive to the fact that she had crossed eyes, posed her head sideways. Lucy Hayes is seen in many pictures seated in a grand, carved wood throne-like chair, worthy of a Victorian First Lady. Still, there was some resistance to all this business. During the 1880 campaign, Lucretia Garfield refused to pose for public

pictures, finally relenting into permitting one portrait of herself to be released. With the 1886 wedding of President Cleveland to 21-year old Frances Folsom, came a great public demand for pictures of the beautiful young bride. By this time, "cabinet" pictures were the vogue (so named because they could be displayed in glass cabinets). They were large photographs, reproduced with a finer quality than the carte de visite cards, and pasted on a sturdy, hard cardboard backing.

Several pictures of Frances Cleveland showed her in the White House – seated in front of the large, semi-circle window that dominates the family quarters, pouring tea in her sunny sitting room. These pictures, however, depended upon natural sunlight. By the beginning of the 20th century, artificial lighting soon made interior photographs possible outside of the studio space. Thus, a First Lady could now pose in the comfort of the White House and the first images of the private quarters began to appear: Ida McKinley in her white bedroom or the oval library, Edith Roosevelt working at her desk in the West Hall, Nellie Taft posed regally in the Green Room. Many an American now glimpsed the family rooms of the White House as they sat back in their own living rooms putting "stereographic cards" into their stereoscopes, and holding them up to their eyes. Curiously, in one photograph of Mrs. McKinley during the 1896 presidential campaign, one can spot a picture from her own collection – of Lucy and Rutherford Hayes.

Public interest in the President and his family reached another peak with the popular Theodore Roosevelts and their children Alice, Theodore, Jr., Kermit, Archie, Ethel, and Quentin. By now, magazines as well as many newspapers, were able to reproduce photographs and the Roosevelts were

MRS. GEN. GRANT.

Carte de visite card of Julia Grant (side view) (top), Images of celebrities such as military, literary and political figures were carried into the homes of average Americans by the carte de visite photograph, an image on paper pasted onto cardboard. These were sold to the general public who often placed them in photo albums along with the reproduced pictures of their own family members. This image in particular shows Julia Grant during the Civil War several years before she became First Lady. Self-conscious of her crossed-eye, she always posed at a side view. In her post-White House years, she had surgery to fix the eye.

Lucy Hayes photographed with new photography technique-halo oval framing (left), Lucy Hayes was popular and widely-known. While she was First Lady, photo technology had progressed to the point where the tedious procedure that used glass plates was obsolete. She posed for dozens of photographs, some of which were processed with new photography techniques such as oval-halo framing.

Stereo-optic viewer (right), **Stereographic card of Frances Cleveland** (middle) The stereographic viewer permitted consumers to view images in three-dimension with what was essentially a trick of the eyes; two frames of the same image were seen by each eye as one placed a photo card in the viewer. Well until the early 1920s, First Ladies were popular subjects for such cards.

4505. Mrs. Frances Cleveland.

regularly featured. Seeking to control what the public glimpsed of herself and her family, Edith Roosevelt controlled the release of pictures to the press and the public, which often wrote for pictures. Like Frances Cleveland and Caroline Harrison before her, Edith Roosevelt permitted Frances Benjamin Johnston, a prominent Washington, D.C. photographer to snap her. Johnston's portraits were artful and appealing to the smart set, and it was her images of the First Ladies that most turn-of-the-century Americans would see.

Also at the beginning of the 20th century, small "brownie" and other portable cameras had become so accessible to the general public as to permit them to to take their own snapshots. The general public, for example, took some of the earliest photographic images of the annual Easter Egg Roll on the White House lawn. First Ladies could not escape progress. Thus – despite their preference for being seen only in posed portraits – Edith Roosevelt was captured on film clumsily climbing onto a horse or Nellie Taft grimly descending a staircase. Early experimentations in color photography

Previously unpublished picture of Caroline Harrison (left),
Previously unpublished image of Mary McElroy (bottom)
Among the rare photography items now in the National First Ladies' Library Audio-Visual Collection are many previously unseen or unknown images of First Ladies, including these two previously unpublished "cabinet card" portraits of Mary "Molly" Arthur McElroy, First Lady to her widowed brother, President Chester Arthur, and of Caroline Harrison.

would capture Edith Wilson standing in the garden with her husband in 1915 and then not again, until 1943 Eleanor Roosevelt seated on the South Lawn with Madame Chiang Kai-Shek. By the end of the long Roosevelt reign, the First Lady, appropriately enough, was one of the first public figures to have her color picture on Time Magazine.

If Americans could not always see their First Ladies in color during the 'Teens, Twenties and Thirties, they could certainly watch them in motion. Beginning with the plentiful newsreel footage taken of President Woodrow Wilson's historic 1919 trip to Europe for the Versailles Treaty, Edith Wilson began to appear as a gesticulating figure besides or behind him as they rode in their open car through European streets, visited American troops still stationed in the battlefields, participated in ceremonies or attended events in palaces. It was her successor Florence Harding, however, who became the first First Lady to appear, regularly and frequently, in newsreels as the primary subject, without the President. Now citizens in the silent movie palaces of the Twenties could see the First Lady tossing dirt with a shovel as she planted a ceremonial tree, or speaking with disabled veterans, or churning a movie camera herself, all with captioned headlines. Her immediate successor Grace Coolidge was in the White House when the first "talkies" came out but - as if out of some sense of compromising the propriety of her First Lady role – she would not permit her voice to be recorded until after her husband's term had ended. Her first "talkie" was as a former First Lady in the fall of 1929 as part of tuberculosis seals drive.

A. Edith Roosevelt mounting horse snapshot (above)

B. Nellie Taft coming down stairs snapshot (below)

Neither Mrs. Harding nor Mrs. Coolidge ever spoke on radio, but Lou Hoover utilized this new technology to address the nation at large and the Girl Scouts of America, specifically, propounding her and the President's views on how voluntarism might help reduce the plight of those families hit hardest by the Great Depression. She even rehearsed her speaking voice in a special room in the White House. Her immediate successor Eleanor Roosevelt used radio to the fullest extent: she became the only First Lady to actually contract with sponsors of her own weekly radio show. Through her Sunday evening talks to the nation for much of her twelve-year tenure as First Lady, her distinctive voice became so familiar to the average American that it was quickly recognized and easily parodied.

As a former First Lady, Mrs. Roosevelt also had her own television show. It was during the Truman and Eisenhower Administrations that television became a permanent fixture in the home of most Americans, but neither First Lady of those Administrations made use of it as a way of addressing the nation. As Mrs. Coolidge had done with talkie newsreels, Bess Truman and Mamie Eisenhower did television interviews only after they had left the White House.

Jacqueline Kennedy most famously appeared on television (through the relatively new technology of videotape) in "A Tour of the White House with Mrs. John F. Kennedy," on CBS-TV on February 14, 1962, yet throughout her whole life did only a handful of brief television interview segments. In contrast, and much to her annoyance, she became unquestionably the most photographed First Lady in history – perhaps even the most photographed woman in the world at one time. Tourists, paparazzi, wire services, official government photographers – Jackie Kennedy seemed perpetually before the camera's lenses, and there are tens of thousands – perhaps

hundreds of thousands – of still pictures chronicling her life.

With Jackie Kennedy, the "official White House photographer" came of age. Initially, Army Signal Corps photographers snapped official and military events at the White House, but soon expanded their duties to include public and private aspects of the lives of the Kennedy family. Lyndon Johnson took an avid interest in having his presidency pictorially chronicled and gave his photographers – especially photojournalist Yoichi Okamoto – unparalleled access to his private life. As a result, private moments of Lady Bird Johnson in her personal rooms were captured and are now preserved at the Lyndon B. Johnson Library in Austin, Texas. Another professional photojournalist, David Kennerly, became a family friend of the Fords. So comfortable with him was Betty Ford that she allowed him to take dozens of pictures of her as she completely relaxed, (even dancing on the Cabinet table) and her years as First Lady are also particularly well chronicled.

As public relations experts within the communications offices of more recent Administrations realized the impact of a single picture, First Ladies became especially powerful subjects for the camera. Thus poignant moments such as Rosalynn Carter ministering to endless rows of Cambodian refugees in a Thailand tent camp, Nancy Reagan placing small flags on the graves of fallen American soldiers of World War II in a misty cemetery at Normandy, or Barbara Bush gently cradling an infant who carried the AIDS virus not only were visually stunning but were meant to convey strong emotions that could very well result in a politically positive message.

It is not the White House photographers alone, however, who have captured some of the most revealing and memorable visual images of the First Ladies. Photographers with international reputations have also come to the White House to work their art on First Ladies at the height of their prominence. In the tradition of Frances Cleveland posing for Frances Johnston, for example, Grace Coolidge sat for Clara Sipprell, Eleanor Roosevelt for Karsch, Jacqueline Kennedy for Cecil Beaton, Mark Shaw and Richard Avedon, Nancy Reagan for Andy Warhol, and Hillary Clinton for Annie Liebowitz.

With the more recent advent of digital still and video cameras and even more instant and improved photography technologies, there is no question that as prominent a figure as a First Lady – or First Gentleman – will be among the first to have their image captured in the most contemporary methods.

Among the first collections archived and made available to the public

C. Bess Truman shopping on street with Margaret snapshot
(above)

A. B. (previous page) **C.** (this page) **D.** (opposite) The "brownie" and other forms of popular portable cameras, often created by the Kodak company, permitted ordinary citizen tourists the chance to snap a candid picture of a First Lady if they happen to spot them around the relatively accessible perimeters of the White House. Although Edith Roosevelt was the first First Lady to issue "official" White House photographs, it did not prevent the proliferation of "candids" showing the presidential spouse in more less-than-monumental moments, unposed and untouched, whether it was Edith Roosevelt trying to mount her horse, Nellie Taft grimacing as she descended a stoop, Bess Truman shopping on a city street with her daughter, or Nancy Reagan walking across Lafayette Square the week after her husband won his 1980 election.

as a reference source and licensing agency at the National First Ladies' Library's Education and Research Center is its audio-visual collection. The hundreds of pictures that I have collected of First Ladies for over three decades will be placed here. Not only are there items I copied from the holdings of other public institutions and archives such as the Library of Congress, and the National Archives' presidential library system, but also the "morgue" collections of defunct newspapers, such as the Cleveland Press, that I was able to purchase. Many of these collections contained not only defunct photo service images, but original photography taken by staff or Washington bureau photographers. Other great finds have also turned up, such as an intimate family picture album from the 1890s of Warren and Florence Harding, which I discovered and purchased at a flea market.

With this large collection as its nucleus, the National First Ladies' Library is even now more active in seeking still photographs as well as portraits, drawings, engravings, cartoons and other forms of images of the First Ladies. In addition, audio recordings, and newsreels, film, videotape, and CD ROMs of moving images will help to make it the national center for both the vocal and visual archive of the First Ladies.

D. Nancy Reagan close-up snapshot candid (below)

Florence Harding and newsreel cameramen capturing her with Filipino women (above) Florence Harding was the first First Lady to willingly "act" for the newsreel cameramen, whose movies were then shown in "motion picture" palaces for the general public to watch as reels were changed for the feature films being shown. Mrs. Harding is seen here on the South Portico with a group of Filipino women seeking independence of their nation.

Cover of book of photographs of Eleanor Roosevelt (right) By the time the activist Eleanor Roosevelt was First Lady, many news agencies were able to transmit still pictures by wire service, permitting widespread newspaper publication of clear images of a First Lady in action. So many pictures were taken of Eleanor Roosevelt that the first photo book chronicling a First Lady's activities was published.

Her Life in Pictures

ELEANOR ROOSEVELT

by Richard Harrity and Ralph G. Martin

Photo courtesy of Ed Clark / Time-Life Pictures / Getty Images

Mamie Eisenhower on cover of Life Magazine (left) By the late Fifties, "Kodachrome" and other color photography techniques were coming into regular use by popular national magazines such as Time, Life, Newsweek and Look. Still, a multi-page spread Life feature offering a glimpse into the various roles of Mamie Eisenhower's life as First Lady was enough of a rarity that it was heralded in the banner on the magazine cover.

Jackie Kennedy on television tour of White House (below) A A full one third of the U.S. population tuned in to watch Jackie Kennedy's famous television tour of the White House on February 14, 1962. Recorded in the new technology of videotape by CBS-TV, it was the first time a First Lady's voice and image were recorded for such a length of time and seen by so many people.

Jackie Kennedy being photographed by paparazzi at airport (left) No First Lady was the subject of more pictures – or more hounded by photographers – than Jackie Kennedy. She is seen here, arriving at an airport for a Greek vacation in 1963, with her sister Princess Lee Radziwill in the foreground, the focus of the Athens "paparazzi."

Pat Nixon and Julie Nixon being filmed while they shop (right) By the 1970s, a First Lady could not only be besieged by the still camera, but the film and video news camera. Here, Pat Nixon and her daughter Julie, try to maintain their composure as the national press closes in on them shopping one Christmas at Sears.

Hillary Clinton being photographed by Annie Liebowitz (above) For over a century now, First Ladies have been popular subjects for what might be termed "art" photographers, who carefully posed, lit and orchestrated their portraits for public consumption, including Clara Sipprell who "did" Grace Coolidge, Karsh of Canada who "did" Eleanor Roosevelt, and Warhol who "did" Nancy Reagan. Here, Annie Liebowitz readies Hillary Clinton for a Vogue Magazine photo shoot.

Photo courtesy of The White House

Laura Bush making weekly radio address (left) First Ladies have been effectively using the radio as a means of addressing the nation on various issues since Lou Hoover did so during the Great Depression. In 2002, however, Laura Bush became the first First Lady to substitute for the President during his weekly Saturday broadcast, speaking out against repression of Afghani women under the Taliban regime.

71

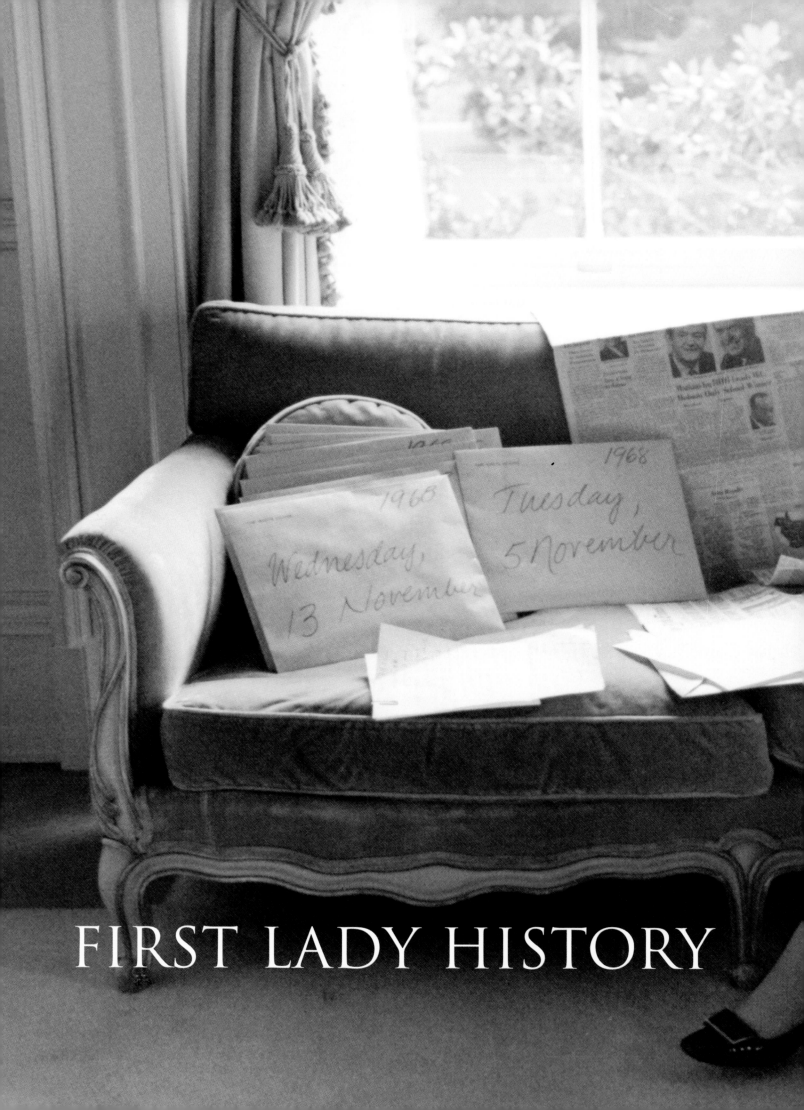

FIRST LADY HISTORY

"...LARGELY SYMBOLIC... LARGELY MYTHICAL..."

First Lady History and a Growing Public Consciousness of Her Role by Carl Sferrazza Anthony, Author and Historian

I would have a "position" but not a real job... There is no training manual for First Ladies... Each carved out a roll that reflected her own interests and style and that balanced the needs of her husband, family and country. So would I... I had to decide what I wanted to do with the opportunities and responsibilities I had inherited. Over the years the roll of First Lady has been perceived as largely symbolic. She is expected to represent an ideal - and largely mythical - concept of American womanhood.

- Hillary Rodham Clinton

Martha Washington as a European queen figure (above) Her portrayal here as a European monarch illustrated how many anti-Federalists viewed Martha Washington in her role as "Lady Washington."

Dolley Madison rescuing Washington's portrait from White House (above)**, "Mrs. Madison" on cover of Port Folio magazine** (right) Dolley Madison became a legend in her own time with her heroic rescue of national treasures from the White House just hours before British troops stormed the capital city and burned the building. She became one of the first famous women in American history and the first First Lady whose image graced the cover of a magazine, in this case the April 1818 issue of *Port Folio*, published in Philadelphia.

Prior to the April 30, 1789 inauguration of George Washington as the first President of the United States, the people of the United States had known of the existence of his wife Martha only as a benevolent general's wife of the American Revolution. The revolutionary soldiers had affectionately dubbed her "Lady Washington," as if she were some sort of quasi-British aristocrat, perhaps an honor to her in light of her presence in their camps and legendary kindness during the bitter winter at Valley Forge that she shared with her husband.

Americans whose ancestors had arrived from Europe all knew of women who had been either rulers in their own right or married to one. At the time of the Washington Inaugural, three entirely different women were exercising various forms of power from throne rooms. Marie Antoinette of France, wife of King Louis, was already being caricatured as a symbol of royal insensitivity to the poor and un-represented peoples of her nation. In Russia, Empress Catherine was openly exercising political and military power in her own right. In England, the mother country of the new United States, Queen Charlotte was still reigning as King George's consort, playing a traditional role as devoted wife to her ailing husband.

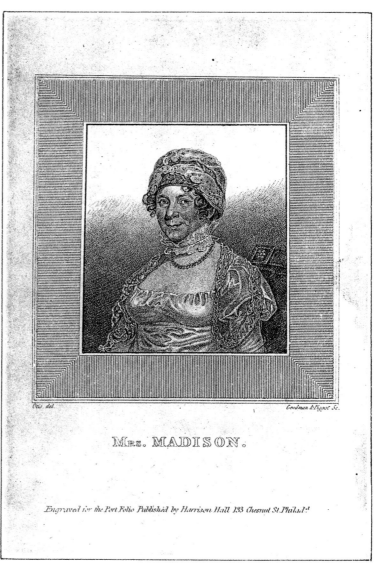

Otis del.   Goodman & Piggot Sc.

Mrs. MADISON.

Engraved for the Port Folio Published by Harrison Hall 133 Chesnut St Philad.

In the United States, which was then composed largely of English-Americans, there was no sense of context to Charlotte's role. She was not compared in any public discourse to, for example, Mary of Orange who had famously co-ruled with her husband William, nor the renowned Elizabeth I, who reigned with more power than most kings did. Only to those aristocrats within the castle walls where portraits of such women hung in halls and stories were passed down the generations was there a sense of continuity to the British queens or kings' consorts. In the general American population, each queen was simply celebrated or despised individually, as if she functioned in a vacuum.

With no consciousness of a cohesive history of the queens of England, it could hardly have been natural for American citizens to view Martha Washington as the first in a line of presidential spouses. The public procession north from his Virginia estate Mount Vernon to the celebration in New York of George Washington's inauguration absolutely marked a new institution in American life - that of the presidency. While part of the sentiment underlining this triumphant procession was based on adoration for General Washington as victor of the American Revolution, the conscious purpose was to witness, honor and cheer him as the new sort of leader of a new sort of government of a new nation. When Martha Washington followed the same path a month later, she was also met with greeting committees, band music, military escort, thirteen-gun salute, receptions and fireworks but as a sort of overdue post-war appreciation for her aid to Revolutionary soldiers. As one newspaper put it, the adulation "recalled the remembrance of those interesting scenes, in which, by her presence, she contributed to relieve the cares of our beloved Chief, and to soothe the anxious moments of his military concern – gratitude marked the recollection, and every countenance bespoke the feelings of affectionate respect." [1] Although honored as a "truly respected personage" and referred to as "Lady Washington" in the *Pennsylvania Packet* newspaper, there were no suggestions in the press that Martha Washington was going to New York to assume a new sort of position, even as hostess of the presidential mansion. [2]

Outside of her being glimpsed entering and exiting her coach during her routine

First commercial print showing grouping of First Ladies together The first bit of material culture that suggests a public consciousness of a sense of continuity to the role of First Lady was this commercially-produced print which groups together First Ladies from Martha Washington to Angelica Van Buren, engravings adapted from their portraits.

"The President's Bride" engraving of Julia Tyler The widespread press coverage of widowed President John Tyler's elopement with the colorful and unusual 24-year old debutante Julia Gardiner provoked a brief but intense interest in her, as evidenced by a mass-produced engraving. Although she is identified as "The President's Bride", she is not mentioned by her name.

Print of Harriet Lane In an 1860 *Leslie's Illustrated* Newspaper article on bachelor President James Buchanan's niece and hostess Harriet Lane that accompanied this engraving of her, the title "First Lady" was used for the first time in print.

shopping trips and social calls in New York and Philadelphia, the second capital city, Martha Washington was only on public view to the press and citizenry at her receptions in the presidential mansions. The formal protocol created by the President's aide Colonel David Humphreys (formerly secretary of the legation at Paris) for these events, Lady Washington was displayed on a slightly raised platform where she received, sometimes seated, sometimes standing. While she was neither in a palace nor seated on a throne, the implication of a watered-down Yankee monarchial form was clear. For the loyal adherents of President Washington's Federalist political party, this vaguely British form seemed appropriate. Some of them had even wanted George Washington to be made King or titled as a demi-royal and thought the President's wife was not treated royally enough. Congressman Thomas Rodney thought that, "In old countries, a Lady of her rank would not be seen without a retinue of twenty persons." [3]

On the other side, however, the anti-Federalists led by Secretary of State Thomas Jefferson, found great fault in such adulation of Lady Washington. Several newspaper editorials considered her receptions anti-democratic. "Levees may be extremely useful in old countries, where men of great fortune are collected…But here I think they are hurtful," Senator William Maclay wrote in his diary, "From these small beginnings I fear we shall follow on nor cease till we have reached the summit of court etiquette, and all the frivolities, fopperies and expense practiced in European governments." [4] Although such commentary was exclusive to Lady Washington's entertaining, it was the first stirring of a public consciousness and debate on the proper role of a President's lady.

The first sense of continuity is suggested by the use of the title "Lady" in reference to the second and third presidential wives to act as their husbands' hostesses, Abigail Adams and Dolley Madison.

At Mrs. Washington's side during her receptions was her friend Abigail Adams, the wife of the Vice President. An overtly partisan Federalist, as the wife of the second president Mrs. Adams was vigorously engaged in the philosophical consideration of government process and political conflict. Thus there was little to compare to her more benign predecessor. Only she compared herself - in a private letter. "As to a crown," she wrote her friend Mercy Otis Warren about Martha Washington, "I shall esteem myself peculiarly fortunate, if, at the close of my public life, I can retire esteemed, beloved and equally respected with my predecessor." [5] As far as the general public, Abigail Adams was treated as a Yankee Queen: a group of Federalists formally called on her, and she presented them with a cockade ribbon, symbol of the party; Native American chiefs came to meet her because, as one said, "duty [was] but in part fulfilled until he had also visited his mother"; others bowed or removed their hats when she passed in the streets. A volunteer light-infantry company even petitioned her to be organized under the name of the "Lady Adams Rangers." [6]

To anti-Federalists, however, she was seen as a partisan symbol of the elite Federalist party. Albert Gallatin said a friend of his "heard her majesty as she was asking the names of different members of Congress and then pointed out which were 'our' people." He dubbed her "Mrs. President, not of the United States but of a faction." [7]

The genuinely first sense that a President's wife was, in some way, a public figure who should have a public profile and act on behalf of the citizens of the nation was Dolley Madison. She had a rare advantage that none of her predecessors or successors had: for a full eight years she was the primary official hostess of the White House under the third President, widower Thomas Jefferson. This was perhaps the most important factor in how she viewed herself as the wife of the fourth President. She consciously used her entertaining in the mansion as an outreach to the political, civic and social communities of Washington and also maintained friendly relations with numerous journalists and writers, who spread the word nationally about her democratic sensibilities.   By permitting all levels of society into her Wednesday night open house receptions, she won the admiration of not only her guests but those around the young nation who read the dispatches of her entertainments, carried and reprinted in regional newspapers and journals. It was her famous act of patriotism in the hours preceding the 1814 burning of the White House by the British, during the War of 1812, that turned her into one of America's first women heroines. Strangers sent her gifts and authors sought her patronage. As the wife of an editor noted, Mrs. Madison was the right person "to dignify the station which she occupies." A banker, one James Barker, named one of his merchant ships Lady Madison. Other titles were even applied to her – "presidentress" and "Lady President." [8]

Like Martha Washington, Dolley Madison was soon immortalized in the popular imagination not as a First Lady but a legendary woman. Neither woman was recalled for activities that were specific to their roles as presidential wives. When they were both among the few women whose likenesses graced the first register of nationally prominent Americans, it was not because they were presidents' wives but legends in their own right. Only a small part of American society – the elite white circles of Washington, and some ripple in those of New York, Boston and other centers along the eastern seaboard – took an interest in, or made note of how a First Lady conducted herself. The uproar over Elizabeth Monroe's decision not to pay social calls was never of interest to the nation at large; it was of intense concern in Washington and in some isolated court circles in Europe. As the Secretary of State's wife, Louisa Adams, wrote from Washington to her father-in-law in Boston, "tastes differ and dear Dolley was much more popular." [9]

The legendary entertaining and popular recognition set by Dolley Madison, however, did emerge as the standard against which subsequent presidential wives were judged. It was during the 1828 campaign that the first suggestion of this standard being applied to a candidate's wife occurred. Rachel Doneslon Robards, the wife of Andrew Jackson married him before obtaining a legal divorce from her first husband and was, technically, a bigamist. Jackson's opposition vigorously exploited this fact as a statement of not only the candidate's character but that of his wife.

Newspaper engraving of Lucy Hayes with Rutherford Hayes on western tour During the Hayes Administration there was a proliferation of "action" images of the popular Lucy Hayes in the nation's illustrated newspaper engravings that portrayed many joint appearances with the President. She is seen here with him during the first presidential trip to the west coast.

Postcard with Frances Cleveland and Martha Washington together Like many of the images of Abraham Lincoln in the period immediately following his assassination that showed him in heaven with George Washington, this picture of Frances Cleveland – who was more well-known across the nation than any of her predecessors – posed her with the sainted image of Martha Washington.

Newspapers such as the *St. Louis Post Dispatch*, *National Banner* and *Nashville Whig* suggested that this potential First Lady was "faithless and worthless." [10]

While no mention of previous First Ladies was made, the underlying message of the anti-Jackson forces was that Rachel Jackson was somehow unqualified to serve as First Lady, thus suggesting that a certain expectation of that role had already been formed in the American mind.

The first documented evidence that any sense of continuity about the First Ladies existed in the larger public mind occurred sometime between 1838 and 1841, when widower President Van Buren's recently wed daughter-in-law Angelica served as his official hostess. In that time, a mass-produced engraving illustrated all the First Ladies since Martha Washington.

The newsworthiness of such an unprecedented event as the marriage of older, widowed President John Tyler, to young, beautiful socialite Julia Gardiner, who was already known in her own right to the New York and Washington press, further prompted a national consciousness of First Ladies. Like Dolley Madison, the newlywed Julia Tyler became a celebrity in her own right – a status she herself perpetuated.

Having recently returned from the courts of Europe, where she met numerous reigning queens and princesses – including the new monarch of the British Empire, Victoria, the 24-year old bride of the President consciously fashioned for herself a public role based on what she had seen overseas. The most striking aspect of this was witnessed by the relatively small number of citizens who came to official events at the White House, where she received with a headpiece that seemed like a crown, while seated in a large throne-like chair on a raised platform. Instead of shaking hands democratically, she nodded to guests whose names were announced in the custom of Buckingham Palace. As a Senator's daughter noted in what was one of the first comparisons made between First Ladies, "Other presidents' wives have taken their state more easily." [11]

Unlike her predecessors, Julia Tyler felt it was her right and responsibility to be seen publicly, and she participated in numerous public ceremonies. She became so well-known by her first name that a New York composer Lovel Purdy wrote a series of dance tunes, "The Julia Waltzes," mass-produced in a first printing of 1,400. The First Lady was quite proud that the dances were "so popular." [12]

For the first time in history, there was frequent and regular coverage of all of the activities of a First Lady through the *New York Herald*. Julia Tyler had calculated it all when she and her brother Alexander befriended a reporter, F.W. Thomas. It was he who sought to officially title the president's wife and, in the process, establish a bona fide public role. He called her "the Presidentress." Not only her name and activities became familiar across the nation, but her image as well. Shortly after her portrait was done, she permitted steel-cut engravings to be made of it, and copies were mass-produced and sold to the public, titled "The President's Bride." The President and Mrs. Tyler certainly had their own ideas on the ideal role of a First Lady. When he met his wife's successor Sarah Polk, John Tyler contrasted her to his own wife. "Imagine," he wrote Julia, "the idea of her being able to follow after you." [13]

Julia Tyler had been First Lady for only eight months, from June 1844 to March 1845, but her publicly conscious role so converged with other events that the notion of a First Lady had been firmly planted in the American mind. Those other events included the very first publication, in 1848, of a book pertaining to a First Lady, *Letters of Mrs. Adams – Wife of John Adams*, compiled and edited by her grandson Charles Francis Adams and, that same year, the Seneca Falls Convention of women who gathered to forment the first organized movement for civil rights of women. In addition, the erudite Sarah Polk followed Mrs. Tyler. Highly educated, well-versed and overtly interested in politics, and serving as a public symbol of support for the American military during the Mexican War, Sarah Polk was, in fact, the first presidential spouse for which there is suggestion that the term "First Lady" might have been used. It is quoted in what is reputed to be an original letter, but appears in a biography that lacks documentation. Still, it could suggest that the expression had been in popular circulation. Another indication that there was a growing public interest in the First Lady as an entity was the reproduction of a colored print of Mrs. Polk that found its way into homes as far away as the southwest territory – despite being mislabeled "Mary – wife of James K. Polk, President of the United States". [14]

Further, Sarah Polk was given material context as a First Lady by her frequent accompaniment at public events by the former First Lady Dolley Madison, then living in Washington as a widow. The visual contrast of the old woman and younger woman inevitably drew comparisons of the two, and imprinted a lasting impression of continuity of First Lady history. This was further solidified when Mrs. Madison and Mrs. Polk were captured in perpetuity together, posing together for a group photograph. Interestingly, also in the photograph was a future First Lady, Harriet Lane, the niece and official White House hostess of the only bachelor President, James Buchanan (1857-1861).

As Americans grew accustomed to the now half-century institution of the presidency, consideration of various aspects of the lives of chief executives expanded. Death notices of obscure First Ladies such as Margaret Taylor, for example, made it into newspapers in 1852 and six months earlier Louisa Adams' death had been reported in the first edition of *The New York Times*. There was detailed reporting on the sudden death of Abigail Fillmore just weeks after she left the role of First Lady in 1853. *The first biographical account of a First Lady* was part of the book *Memoirs of the Mother and Wife of Washington* by Margaret Conkling in 1850. Upon Sarah Polk's retirement, a tribute poem to her years in the White House appeared in the March 1849 issue of *Peterson's Magazine*.

The term "First Lady" was first used in the public press in reference to Harriet Lane in the March 21, 1860 edition of *Leslie's Illustrated Newspaper*. Its use may have been intended to make a distinction between a president's wife who served as hostess and a relative, like Miss Lane, who served as hostess, as if the latter was of a reduced status, or simply to officially desig-

Fanciful view of Martha Washington comforting George Washington (opposite) As the nation celebrated the centennial of George Washington's inauguration, in 1889, and the four-hundredth anniversary of the Columbus discovery of America, in 1892, patriotic fervor ignited romanticized versions of the heroes and heroines of the early Republic. Not only did the first biographies of Martha Washington and Dolley Madison begin to appear, but many color illustrations of fanciful moments in their lives were created for popular and women's magazines, such as this homey depiction of the first First Couple in *Ladies Home Journal*.

nate a sort of leading female head of the nation. A further distinction in the connotation that such a woman had a national profile and role was in the use of the fuller expression, "First Lady of the land," as opposed to "mistress of the White House," the latter suggesting traditional household responsibilities. Whatever the motivation in using the term, it stuck, and it was used in reference to Lane's successor, Mary Todd Lincoln in at least one paper, the *Sacramento Union* on December 4, 1863.

Mary Todd Lincoln also added a new dimension to the popular ideas about what a First Lady should or should not do. When she traveled through the Northeast with Lincoln in the pre-Inaugural period and openly discussed politics, one incredulous politician observed that, "Mrs. Lincoln's journey is considered very much out of place, the idea of the President's wife kiting about the country and holding levees at which she indulges in a multitude of silly speeches is looked upon as very shocking…" [15]

In the midst of the Civil War, Mrs. Lincoln was a victim as much of regional acrimony as her own determination to reign splendidly. While her southern background provided fodder for a suspicious anti-Lincoln press, it was her entertaining lavishly and seeming self-indulgence in clothing and material luxury during wartime, as well as her volunteer activities as First Lady that prompted frequent editorial comment, with a slight suggestion of hostility yet still respecting a sort of chivalrous code of not attacking a woman in the public print. "Others occupying the same high position," the *New York Herald* noted wryly, "have failed to excite a similar interest." The *Springfield Massachusetts Republican*, a newspaper friendly to the President, suggested that this first overtly political First Lady was operating unlike any of her predecessors: "Her friends compare Mrs. Lincoln to Queen Elizabeth in her statesmanlike tastes and capabilities…She has ere this made and unmade the political fortunes of men…Nothing escapes her eye." [16]

What was noteworthy about this, in terms of First Lady history, was that it marked the first time a First Lady was considered to be publicly accountable enough to merit public censure.

While newspaper articles on Julia Grant focused her domestic life and entertaining, the first public notice of a First Lady playing a political role in a specific situation was suggested in the *New York Herald* after Interior Secretary Jacob Cox resigned under fire. This, the newspaper noted, was partly due to "little disagreements and unpleasantness in the female department…" [17]

The acknowledgement of a First Lady having political influence was presented not yet as a criticism, but rather as a humorously quaint reference to the inevitable "meddling" of a woman in man's work. When Lucy Hayes was away from her husband in the White House, one newspaper whimsically noted that, "Mr. Hayes will, during the absence of Mrs. Hayes, be acting President…" [18] It would be some forty more years, in 1919, before the political influence of a First Lady became a provocative matter of national debate.

That Lucy Hayes was so regularly featured in the national press – even

Group engraving of all the First Ladies By the beginning of the 19th century, the very concept of "First Ladies" as an historical continuum had firmly entered the national consciousness as this imaginative 1902 group rendering of them all illustrates.

Title page and picture from book "First Lady of the Land" (top), **Photo of Nellie Taft Inaugural gown in Smithsonian case, 1912** (bottom) During the Taft Administration, national consciousness of the First Ladies was further solidified by two events. The Broadway run of a comedy play about Dolley Madison, based on a novel (the title page seen above) the title of which, "First Lady of the Land," was widely spread into the mainstream. In 1912, Nellie Taft became the first incumbent First Lady to donate her gown to the new Smithsonian collection of First Lady gowns - seen here in its original display case. The permanent exhibit remains one of the most popular sites for visitors to the nation's capital.

caricatured in cartoon – was due to the edict of the White House that no alcoholic beverages would be served to guests. Although, in fact, it had been a political decision made by the President to maintain support of the Prohibition Party, it was popularly depicted as a domestic decision that came, naturally, under the First Lady's responsibilities. Her frequent presence in the nation's newspaper columns as "First Lady of the land" may have firmly established that title in the national lexicon, but it also led later historians to mistakenly claim that the title originated with Mrs. Hayes.

More than any of her predecessors, Lucy Hayes took a personal interest in the history of First Ladies and may, in fact, have been the first one to be so conscious of it at all. When she toured the South with the President, Mrs. Hayes made a point of paying homage to her elderly predecessor Sarah Polk, a widow in Nashville. Although the former First Lady Julia Tyler has been credited with starting the White House's collection of First Lady portraits, she had simply donated her own with the hopes of it being hung and being remembered; it was Lucy Hayes who had posthumous portraits of Martha Washington and Dolley Madison commissioned for the White House.

The publicity generated by Lucy Hayes, as well as the coverage of the lobbying for a presidential widow's pension to Congress by "Mrs. Ex-President Tyler" stirred up enough attention on the subject of First Ladies that the first collected biographies of the First Ladies, along with steel-cut engravings, was published in 1880. Laura C. Holloway's *Ladies of the White House; or, in the Home of the Presidents - Being a Complete History of the Social and Domestic Lives of the Presidents from Washington to the Present Time* and its updated edition in 1882 (under her married name, Langford), became the standard work on the subject for generations. Holloway was the first person to conduct serious and in-depth research on the First Ladies, contacting grandchildren and children of First Ladies and the several living former First Ladies, visiting presidential homes and quoting from letters.

Several First Ladies themselves were now keenly aware of their "heritage," so to speak, and a new custom began during the tenure of Mary McElroy, the sister and hostess of widowed President Chester Arthur. She honored former First Ladies Harriet Lane and Julia Tyler by inviting them to receive with her. Subsequent First Lady Frances Cleveland also invited the two former First Ladies as well as Lucretia Garfield to receptions and dinners. While interest and coverage of the return of the former First Ladies was limited largely to the Washington area, it elevated these women who had once lived in the White House into national celebrities. Considerable press coverage was spurred about them. Julia Tyler even granted several newspaper interviews. Citizens no longer wrote to presidential widows seeking clipped signetures of their late husbands - but of the First Ladies them-

Lady Bird Johnson in her office on telephone with secretary
(above) As head of her own radio station, Lady Bird Johnson knew how vital a well-organized staff was to efficiency. She was the first First Lady to have a structured East Wing staff, including those who handled "advance," "press," "social events," "correspondence," and "special projects." Under Mamie Eisenhower and Jackie Kennedy, a "Social Secretary" had been expected to oversee everything.

Grace Coolidge and her Secret Service agent Jim Haley
(opposite) Florence Harding was the first First Lady to make use of a federally-funded protective agent. It was Grace Coolidge, however, who was first identified with her Secret Service agent Jim Haley by the public and press, as he accompanied her on the streets of Washington and other places she visited where she took her famous walks and hikes. A ludicrous press romance was even suggested as existing between the First Lady and Haley.

selves.

A gauge of the growing national interest in First Ladies was both mirrored and perpetuated by the era's two leading illustrated weekly newspapers, *Harper's* and *Leslie's*. Harriet Lane, Mary Lincoln, Julia Grant and Lucy Hayes were frequently pictured in pen drawings capturing them attending ceremonies or other activities as well as in portraits. The 1881 shooting and lingering of President James Garfield provided citizens not only with its first visual glimpses of the private White House rooms but almost weekly drawings and reports illustrating how bravely Lucretia Garfield was managing. Editorials praised her as a role model for all American women and after the President's death, she was so well-known and admired that a large national collection of funds provided considerable material comfort for the rest of her and her children's lives.

If Americans now had a stronger sense of their First Ladies, certain spectacular and unusual events involving a president's wife only intensified that interest. No First Lady up to that time became as well-known as quickly as Frances Cleveland, when the 21 year old delightfully shocked the nation by marrying the 54 year old bachelor President Grover Cleveland in the White House on June 2, 1886. In the industrial age of mass-production, "Frankie" Cleveland's image was pasted on all types of products and advertising, and even her honeymoon was minutely covered in the daily press, with endless picture drawings and seemingly endless columns filled with every possible detail. Her age, and the unusual circumstance of her rise to the role of First Lady captured the imagination of newspaper and magazine editors and reporters and, consequently, the public. In turn, it again provoked an overall interest in all of the First Ladies. A second book of collective biographies of First Ladies, *From Lady Washington to Mrs. Cleveland*, was hastily churned out by one Lydia Gordon, and filled with numerous inaccuracies and even the misspelling of Ellen Arthur as "Ella."

Among the many souvenir postcards depicting Mrs. Cleveland was one that paired a saintly image of the first First Lady, Martha Washington, in the background of the young president's bride. Use of the expression "First Lady" was constant in reference to Mrs. Cleveland. This was particularly offensive to the President, who genuinely viewed his wife as an entirely private person and not a public figure in any sense. "I have my heart set upon making Frank a sensible, domestic American wife and would be pleased not to hear her spoken of as 'The First Lady of the Land.'" [19]

Nevertheless, the public remained fixated on Frances Cleveland and, she was the most widely known and popular First Lady since Dolley Madison. It is therefore perhaps no coincidence that *Memoirs and Letters of Dolley Madison*, written by the former First Lady's niece Lucia Cutts was published the year of the Cleveland wedding, and that a second biography of Dolley Madison, by Maude Wilder Goodwin, was published at the end of the second Cleveland term, in 1896. That same year, during the presidential campaign, one women's magazine even ran articles on the two prospective First Ladies, Ida McKinley and Mary Bryan.

In the twentieth century, national interest in the history of First Ladies

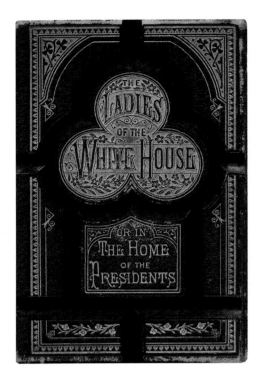

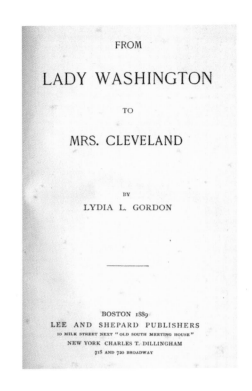

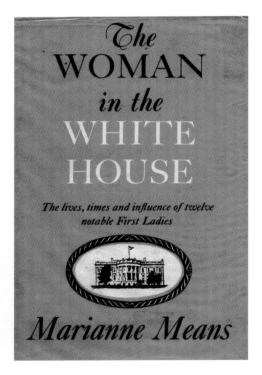

Cover of "The Presiding Ladies of the White House" (top left), **Title page of "From Lady Washington to Mrs. Cleveland"** (top right), **Cover of "First Ladies" by Prindiville** (bottom left), **Cover of "The Woman in the White House"** (bottom right) The first collective biographies of First Ladies, *The Presiding Ladies of the White House*, took a predictably Victorian perspective on their roles, focusing on their domesticity, yet also drawing from family recollections and letters. The book included new First Ladies in succeeding editions. *From Lady Washington to Mrs. Cleveland* served a more political purpose, portraying First Ladies in the context of their husbands' careers and providing more biographical data about the Presidents than about their wives. By the mid-twentieth century, legend and romanticization heavily influenced the portrayals of these women in polite books such as Kathleen Prindiville's *First Ladies*; it chivalrously sought to shine a glowing light on each woman and avoid difficult moments or unpleasant truths in their lives. In 1962, *The Woman in the White House* became the first book to consider a dozen First Ladies with an honest viewpoint, focusing not only on their traditional roles but also their political influence. Presidents Truman, Eisenhower and Kennedy all granted personal interviews in which they were questioned about their First Lady's roles.

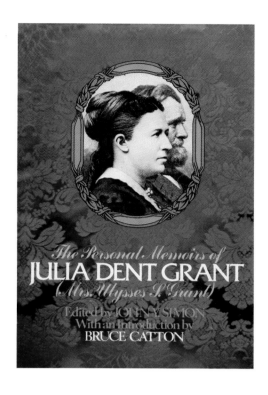

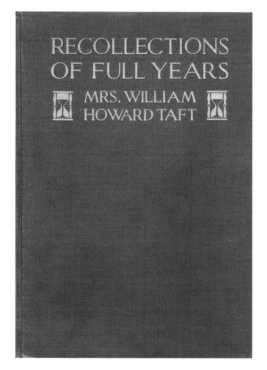

Cover of Julia Grant's memoirs (top left), **Cover of Helen Taft's memoirs** (bottom left), **Lady Bird Johnson tape-recording her daily diary** (top right), **Barbara Bush typing her diary on a computer** (bottom right) The first First Lady to write her memoirs was Julia Grant, but it was felt that her assessments of many leading political figures of the day was too frank to be coming from a woman. Her book was posthumously published a full century after she was in the White House. Nellie Taft was the first to publish her autobiography, *Recollections of Full Years*, in 1914. Lady Bird Johnson assiduously kept to a daily diary of her White House years that she tape-recorded. It was later edited and published as *A White House Diary*. Barbara Bush also kept a diary of her public life, but she wrote it herself on a computer, the first First Lady to use this technology. Her memoirs became a national best-seller.

waxed and waned according to the prominence of First Ladies in the news. After the 1902 renovation of the White House under Theodore Roosevelt, reporter Abby Gunn Baker covered details on the household and decorating changes instituted by Edith Roosevelt. Her series of articles prompted interest in the subject from Washington correspondents of regional papers. Baker paid especial attention to the collection of china used by past First Ladies that Mrs. Roosevelt gathered in hutches for display, as well as the placement of all portraits of past First Ladies in the new ground floor hallway. For the first time in the White House there was a conscious and now visual sense of continuity of First Ladies. This, in turn, prompted the third book of collective biographies of First Ladies, *Ladies of the White House* by Margaret Sangster, each with a large engraving. First Lady history had permanently taken hold even in the class rooms, where Martha Washington's picture invariably hung along with George's.

The simple symbolic act of Helen "Nellie" Taft insisting on riding with her husband after his inaugural in an open carriage – an honor previously bestowed on male officials – garnered tremendous public attention, usually with the remark that she was "the first" First Lady to do so. The idea of First Ladies setting new precedents and each having high public profiles was strongly established with the women who held the position in the early twentieth century. Nellie Taft, Ellen Wilson and Edith Wilson (the first and second wives of President Woodrow Wilson), and Florence Harding were each formidable figures who made news in their own right. Nellie Taft was the first First Lady to publish her memoirs in 1914; Ellen Wilson was the first to lobby on behalf of Congressional legislation; Edith Wilson, following her husband's stroke, covertly administered the presidency and it became public knowledge at the time; Florence Harding, the first First Lady to vote, spoke out

Lou Hoover at her desk in the private quarters (top), **Rosalynn Carter at her desk in the East Wing** (middle) Until the late 20th century, First Ladies (like Lou Hoover above) conducted their role from a desk and makeshift office in the private family rooms. Rosalynn Carter was the first to maintain her own office with her staff in the East Wing. Hillary Clinton has been the only First Lady thus far to keep an office in the West Wing.

frequently on issues of women's equality.

First Ladies had become newsworthy figures throughout the nation, no longer just in Washington, D.C. Thus when Grace Coolidge and Lou Hoover, (who avoided all controversy) presided at various civic events and ceremonies, they were in the news the next day. Comparative articles began to appear about the First Ladies in national newspapers and women's magazines, either profiling all those who were alive at any given moment or analyzing them in the published reminiscences of various Washington figures who knew several of them.

Perhaps no more permanent sense of First Lady history was preserved for the nation than the popular Smithsonian exhibition of their gowns, Starting in 1912. Books, articles, pamphlets, postcards, paper dolls and costumed figurines were published and manufactured, copying the gowned mannequins, starting in the 1920s. An actual trip to the nation's capital was no longer required for a citizen to visually imagine a long, unbroken line going back to the first First Lady. If the women were compared and contrasted, however, it was only in the context of their fashion styles. So strong was this impulse that it persisted even during the unprecedented twelve-year tenure of Eleanor Roosevelt. No matter how political or controversial Eleanor Roosevelt might be, she was always portrayed in traditional terms (fashion, entertaining, family life) when presented in the context of her predecessors. Otherwise, the contrast between this activist First Lady who had no hesitation in appearing in public in her riding jodhpurs or other informal clothing, and her predecessors in frilly, colorful gowns was stark. This visual discord played out in the ongoing public dialogue about what was the "right" role for

Nancy Reagan with international First Ladies at 1985 UN Conference (below) Nancy Reagan accompanied her husband to every nation he visited – except a short trip to Iceland. Consequently, many nations that had no paradigm for the very concept of "First Lady" often found that the wives of their leaders were making a first or rare public appearance at welcoming and other ceremonies that required an equal of sorts to welcome Mrs. Reagan. When she hosted a United Nations conference on drug abuse, several international "First Ladies" who attended suddenly found themselves public figures for the first time in their home nations.

a First Lady throughout the Roosevelt Administration. Even the popular and young adult biographies on Martha Washington, Abigail Adams, Dolley Madison and Mary Lincoln which appeared in the 1930s and 1940s resisted making any parallels to the unusual woman then presiding in the White House. With Bess Truman and Mamie Eisenhower as First Ladies in the latter 1940s and the 1950s, there was a sense from the romanticized First Lady literature of the time that these two momen had somehow restored the role of First Lady to its "proper" function. China patterns, favorite food recipes, hat and clothing fashions, interior decorating and entertaining styles were the stuff of First Lady history in post-war America. While the arrival of such an unusually young and urbane woman as Jacqueline Kennedy to the role of First Lady in 1961 prompted a new burst of interest in First Lady history, it remained essentially focused on those traditional aspects of White House hostess.

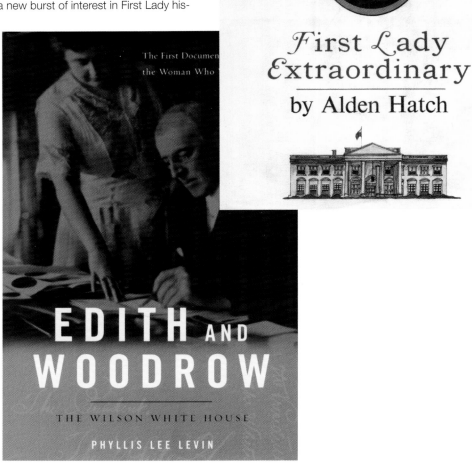

Biographies of past First Ladies appearing in the late 1950s and 1960s only underlined this fixation. Although authored by a credible *New York Times* reporter Ishbel Ross, her biographies of Grace Coolidge, Julia Grant and - as a small part of a larger family history - Nellie Taft, nevertheless dwelt on seemingly incidental facts. In contrast, Robert Seager's 1962 joint biography of John Tyler and Julia Tyler, *And Tyler Too*, was the first scholarly and documented portrayal of a First Lady that covered her entire life in detail since Ruth Painter Randall's 1953 *Mary Lincoln: Biography of a Marriage* (the first book to make full use of the Lincoln papers, only opened in 1948). Young, glamorous, Long Island socialite and later Catholic convert, Julia Tyler was a natural subject with Jackie Kennedy in the White House.

In that it was also a joint biography of a President, the Seager book gave readers a President's wife who proved to be as interested in politics as she was in clothing. In one regard the book also raised questions – what if it had not been a joint look? Would a biography of such an obscure but interesting First Lady like Julia Tyler simply ignore the full breadth of her political letters? In the eyes of Jackie Kennedy herself, there was resistance to viewing First Ladies as being worthy of consideration apart from the Presidents. Not only did she strongly dislike the title "First Lady" but she felt that her hus-

Cover of "Edith Wilson: First Lady Extraordinaire" by Alden Hatch, 1961 (top), **Cover of "Edith and Woodrow" by Phyllis Lee Levin 2001** (middle) The preservation of First Lady papers by the National Archives' presidential library system, the Library of Congress and many other institutions, in conjunction with a growing respect for scholarship of First Lady history that began in the 1980s is helping to redefine many of the First Ladies and clarify misperceptions about them. A biography of Edith Wilson written while she was alive, for example, was done only with her cooperation and veto power over her biographer's use of her papers. It now stands in contrast to a starkly honest biography of her written forty years later that was based on full access to her papers and was the first to fully document her controversial political role.

band should somehow be credited for her restoration project. Not until many years later, as Mrs. Onassis, did she feel comfortable acknowledging the full value and impact of her own work and efforts during the Kennedy Administration.

In 1963, a year after Eleanor Roosevelt's death and a month before the assassination of President Kennedy, the first book to ever consider the varying degrees of personal influence and public impact of First Ladies was published. *The Woman in the White House*, by the Hearst newspaper chain's White House correspondent Marianne Means, was a marked departure from previous collective biographies. It chose twelve "women" among First Ladies, suggesting individualistic personalities of consequence who left legacies within their husbands' presidencies: Martha Washington, Abigail Adams, Dolley Madison, Sarah Polk, Mary Lincoln, Nellie Taft, Edith Wilson, Florence Harding, Eleanor Roosevelt, Bess Truman, Mamie Eisenhower and Jackie Kennedy. Without making a value judgment on what was the best way a First Lady should conduct herself, Means showed that not only overt political involvement, but subtle emotional control were venues that First Ladies had used to leave their mark on the presidency. The book anticipated the changing view of First Lady history by the next generations.

The women's movement for equal rights that entered the mainstream consciousness in America at the end of the 1960s and throughout the 1970s greatly shifted the focus of First Lady history. Highly readable yet serious in scope, *Eleanor and Franklin* (1971) by Roosevelt friend Joseph P. Lash, presented the familiar figure of Eleanor Roosevelt behind the scenes, having a genuine impact on numerous aspects of American life – government and politics, equal rights for women and minorities, and general social history and popular culture. Further, Mrs. Roosevelt's accomplishments were proven with detailed documentation from materials in the Roosevelt Presidential Library.

In the context of America's 1976 Bicentennial, First Lady Betty Ford fighting for passage of the Equal Rights Amendment, Democratic presidential candidate Jimmy Carter's wife Rosalynn promising to carry out her own agenda of mental health and senior citizen legislation reform and the creation of many "women's studies" departments at major universities, the history of First Ladies took a new direction. With overtly political First Ladies like Betty Ford and Rosalynn Carter involving themselves in controversial political and social issues of the times, historians and journalists alike seemed more interested in beginning to chronicle the contributions of their predecessors in areas other than the traditional arenas of entertaining, decorating and clothing. In the first edition (1975) of the White House Historical Association's *First Ladies*, for example, an effort was made by its author, Smithsonian curator Margaret Klapthor to include mention of the accomplishments, influences, work, projects and intellectual pursuits of the First Ladies. That same year, the memoirs penned nearly a century earlier by Julia Grant, but withheld from publication because it showed her to be more political than was thought seemly for ladies at the time, were finally, posthumously published.

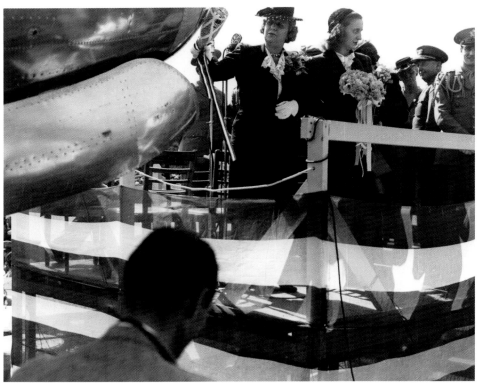

Eleanor Roosevelt and the Queen of England (opposite top), **Bess Truman christening airplane** (opposite bottom), **Hillary Clinton at Easter Egg Roll** (top), **Barbara Bush placing star on top of Christmas tree** (bottom) Whether an "activist" First Lady has preceded or succeeded a "traditionalist" one, they have all recognized the public relations value of continuing to participate in what has become rituals and customs long associated with First Ladies – such as presiding over holiday events, cutting ribbons, christening ships or planes, or chaperoning visiting dignitaries. Despite her highly controversial political role, for example, Eleanor Roosevelt still honored the First Lady ceremonial role, not unlike the one played by the Queens of England such as Elizabeth, seen here visiting Washington in 1939.

A. Fords

In the 1980s, genuine scholarship on the First Ladies was only now beginning, with the papers of First Ladies starting to become available in the archives of presidential libraries, a system which extended back the Herbert Hoover presidency. Collections of earlier First Ladies papers in the Library of Congress and other institutions were finally being studied and used not for background information on Presidents, but as the basis for studies on the women themselves. In that decade, new biographies of Mary Lincoln, Abigail Adams, Lucy Hayes, Edith Roosevelt, Bess Truman, Pat Nixon and Louisa Adams were published, based on primary sources including family letters, diaries and official documents. In the fall of 1982, American history professor Lewis Gould taught University of Texas at Austin students in the first college course ever given on First Ladies and a year later, former First Lady Betty Ford hosted the first symposium on First Ladies, even participating in a panel with Rosalynn Carter. At a 1984 Hunter College centennial tribute to Eleanor Roosevelt, the first scholarly conference on First Ladies was held. In that same period, Siena College conducted a poll among presidential historians seeking to rate the First Ladies comparing them in various categories, despite the fact that for most of those being judged there was little but anecdotal and apocryphal information on them readily available.

The firing of Reagan Chief of Staff Donald Regan and the extent to which Nancy Reagan was involved seized headlines and international attention in February 1987 and stimulated media interest in the history of First Ladies as reporters sought, for the first time, to provide historical context to what was initially assumed to be an unprecedented situation. Closer scrutiny was given to Mrs. Reagan's role as an unofficial advisor to her husband, especially after a scathing editorial by a partisan supporter of the President, *New York Times* columnist William Safire, in which he compared the First Lady to "an incipient Edith Wilson, unelected and unaccountable, presuming to control the actions and appointments of the executive branch." [20] At the very least, it was contemporary evidence that a First Lady who had

B. Carters

C. Reagans

been assumed to be interested only in the traditional role could, through crisis and rising circumstances, assume a role of political consequence. In reaction, Mrs. Reagan, in her memoirs, was flatly honest about her vital role in her husband's presidency. This followed equally frank memoirs of Betty Ford (1978) and Rosalynn Carter (1984). By 1990, the Smithsonian had decided to replace its dated yet still-popular exhibit of First Lady gowns with a richer exhibit exploring the various components of a First Lady's role – political, symbolic, social and even commercial. It was dedicated in 1992. By this time several new books specifically analyzing the impact of First Ladies had been published.

If Mrs. Reagan occasionally made controversial headlines and her successor Barbara Bush made even less, their successor Hillary Rodham Clinton was constantly, sometimes daily, a figure of international media attention. No First Lady and her work had ever been as fully integrated into the presidency and been so viable a target for political opponents. In many ways, the eight years of Hillary Clinton's tenure were a series of test cases on how the role of First Lady could be expanded, and at what cost, beginning with the President asking her to chair his Health Care Reform initiative to her election as a United States Senator in her own right. However unprecedented, elements of Mrs. Clinton's tenure were often given historical context, the public record of all First Ladies having been increased considerably since, for example, Eleanor Roosevelt's controversial tenure. Thus, Hillary Clinton's chairing of health care reform was compared to Rosalynn Carter's chairing on mental health reform. Implication of her offices in political scandal was compared to those involving Julia Grant and a Wall Street scandal. Her intellectual partnership with the President conjured numerous comparisons – John and Abigail Adams, James and Sarah Polk, Will and Nellie Taft and, of course, Franklin and Eleanor Roosevelt. Even Hillary Clinton's placement of contemporary American crafts and a modern sculpture garden had parallels in Jackie Kennedy's promotion and support of experimental and abstract art of the mid-20th century.

While her staff fully utilized the sources available on First Lady history to place Mrs. Clinton in historical context, she herself took a direct interest in how she was expanding the choices for her successors, just as some of her predecessors had done for her. Perhaps just as revealing of Mrs. Clinton's confidence in her role in the wake of frequent controversy was her avid interest and knowledge of First Lady history, notably the lives of Dolley Madison and Eleanor Roosevelt. Along with Nancy Reagan, Barbara Bush and Rosalynn Carter, Hillary Clinton participated in a twelve-week symposium, "The President's Spouse," hosted by George Washington University in the autumn of 1994, discussing not only her interpretation of the First Lady role but the historical evolution of it. Her early belief in the value of First Lady history was a vital factor in the founding and creation of the National First Ladies' Library in 1997.

As differently as Laura Bush may interpret her role as First Lady, she also evidenced a great love of history and knowledge of predecessors, naming Lady Bird Johnson and her environmental protection work, for example,

D. Bushes

as a particular point of interest and personal admiration. During the Clinton years, new scholarly biographies and edited letter collections of even less-known First Ladies such as Sarah Polk, Florence Harding and Mamie Eisenhower were published, underscoring that even among the more obscure, all First Ladies influenced their husbands and, as a result, history. A University of Hawaii professor began efforts to have biographies of all the First Ladies compiled, and there was even a book published on the premise that presidential-marriages-as-partnerships were unsuccessful, written by a Canadian professor.

Research and new works in First Lady history continue during Laura Bush's tenure. *Edith & Woodrow* by Phyllis Lee Levin, an explosively revealing study of Edith Wilson's controversial role as "the first woman president," during her husband's stroke, was finally published in 2001 based on primary sources and other previously untapped materials. That same year, a plethora of books on Jacqueline Kennedy appeared, several specializing on distinct aspects of her life. There are also biographies and collected letters anticipated of Dolley Madison, Lucretia Garfield, Nellie Taft, and Eleanor Roosevelt, as well as Hillary Clinton's memoirs. The ceremonial gathering of living First Ladies, a custom in frequent practice by the 1990s at presidential library dedications and funerals, even occurred at one of the most tragic moments in American history, the attack on September 11, 2001 by terrorists. Attending a National Cathedral memorial service for those who died that day were Betty Ford, Rosalynn Carter, Barbara Bush, Hillary Clinton and Laura Bush, with their husbands. The tableaux of such a gathering provided a visual continuity and sense of stability for the mourning nation, the event planned by Laura Bush. The same group, minus Laura Bush but including Lady Bird Johnson, had gathered less than a year before at the Clinton state dinner for the bicentennial of the White House. Four former First Ladies – Rosalynn Carter, Nancy Reagan, Barbara Bush and Hillary Clinton – gathered to honor Betty Ford on the 20th anniversary of the Betty Ford Center in January 2003.

In the coming years, the National First Ladies' Library promises to be

E. Clintons

F. George W. Bushes

the nation's most important center of study for First Lady history. Whether it be for historians or schoolchildren, the mission will be the same – to highlight the lives and contributions of the First Ladies and illustrate just how vital their story has been to the national one.

A – F (pages 94-100) Since the era of the "women's liberation movement," more men and women have been acknowledged as sharing the burden of family responsibilities and decisions. This shift in perception has been reflected in the more natural and informal presentation of First Ladies as part of a team with their husband-Presidents. For the first time, First Couples were frequently pictured hugging, touching, kissing and holding hands. Seen on pages 94-100 are the Fords, Carters, Reagans, Bushes, Clintons and Bushes.

[1] *Pennsylvania and Daily Advertiser*, May 26, 1789

[2] *Pennsylvania Packet*, May 26, 1789

[3] Anthony, v. 1, p. 48

[4] journal of Pennsylvania Senator William Maclay, reprinted in Mary Caroline Crawford, *Romantic Days in the Early Republic* (Boston: Little Brown, 1912), p. 85

[5] Abigail Adams to Mercy Otis Warren, March 4, 1797, quoted in Laura E. Richards, *Abigail Adams and Her Times* (New York: Appleton, 1917) pp. 248-249

[6] Anthony, p. 63; Charles Akers, *Abigail Adams* (Boston: Little Brown, 1980), pp. 153, 161

[7] Lynne Withey, *Dearest Friend: A Life of Abigail Adams* (New York: Free Press, 1981) p. 254; Page Smith, *John Adams*, (New York: Doubleday, 1962) volume 2, p. 937

[8] Anthony, pp. 83-84; Elizabeth Seaton diary entry of January 2, 1814, quoted in Allen Clark, *Life and Letters of Dolley Madison* (Washington: W.F. Roberts, 1914) pp. 157-158, 403; use of term "presidentress," *National Intelligencer*, March 4, 1809. Senator Samuel Mitchell of New York, however, used the expression in a letter to his wife on January 25, 1808. He also used the term "Lady President in a letter of November 23, 1807, see Clark, 91, 93

[9] Louisa Adams to John Adams, March 2, 1818, Adams Papers, Massachusetts Historical Society

[10] quoted from pamphlet of speech defending Rachel Jackson made by Thomas Kennedy on August 4, 1827, cited in Mary French Caldwell, *General Jackson's Lady* (Nashville: Kingsport Press, 1936), pp. 411-412

[11] Jessie Benton Fremont, *Souvenirs of My Time* (Boston: D. Lothrop & Co., 1887), p. 99

[12] Julia Tyler to Juliana Gardiner, December 1844, Gardiner Family Papers, Yale University

[13] Seager, pp. 283, 263-264, 333

[14] *Recollections of Elizabeth Benton Fremont*, (New York: Frederick Hitchcock, 1912) p. 15

[15] Anthony, volume 1, p. 169

[16] Anthony, volume 1, *New York Herald* quoted on p. 175 and *Springfield Massachusetts Republican* quoted on pp. p. 180-181

[17] *New York Herald*, November 5, 1870

[18] Anthony, p. 231

[19] Grover Cleveland to Mary Hoyt, March 21, 1886, as cited in Allan Nevins, ed., *Letters of Grover Cleveland, 1850-1908* (Boston: Houghton Mifflin, 1933)

[20] *New York Times*, March 2, 1987

"...US WOMEN..."

First Ladies and Women's History by Carl Sferrazza Anthony, Author and Historian

> Men have the advantage of us women,
>
> in being able to go out in the world and earn a living.
>
> -Mary Lincoln

Abigail Adams – young picture from Revolutionary era on collectible plate (above) Abigail Adams was one of the first women in the United States to support equal rights for women in education, and politics. As First Lady, however, she viewed women's role much more traditionally than she had as the young radical revolutionary wife of a member of the Continental Congress during the War For Independence.

At a glance, the First Ladies seem to be one of the most homogeneous groupings of women in American history: white Protestant English-American women of wealth and privilege, removed from the mundane worries and responsibilities of the "average American woman." Certainly, life in the White House – even in the 19th century – provided that no woman would be responsible for cleaning and cooking or be denied any necessities, even if one's husband was cash poor. It is also true that most of them, by the time their husbands became President, could live in the creature comforts of a closed and choice society. If they wished, they did not even have to look at slaves or servants ordering them out of sight.

If one studies their full lives, however, they become a vastly different group, each of them more dissimilar than alike. And, in considering the issues they faced as private women, as well as those issues they might willingly address as public women, the lives of the First Ladies track remarkably with the larger movements of American women's history: from property rights to abolition and slavery to women's suffrage to higher education for women to temperance to protective labor reform, to civic and political involvement to the fight for equal rights legislation.

If the general public knows any fact about Martha Washington beyond her being a general's wife and First Lady it is that, she was a wealthy widow when George Washington married her. Yet encapsulated within that fact is that she was not only versed in the business aspects of her vast inherited real estate holdings, but also had a working knowledge of animal husbandry,

Dolley Madison black-and-white portrait with turban (right) Dolley Madison insisted on bringing women into the halls of Congress and the Supreme Court to listen to debates and speeches and learn more about government. Always sitting in the visitors' gallery, she was later given an honorary seat on the floor of Congress.

herbal medicines, agricultural sciences and, essentially – when one considers the large number of slaves, servants and others she oversaw at Mount Vernon in the absence of her husband – personnel management. Women's property rights in the early 19th century are further told in the stories of First Ladies who inherited wealth, either from their fathers or first husbands, and added substantially to the financial foundation of their husbands – enough so, in some instances, as to permit them to pursue careers in public service and seek the presidency. Further, test cases on inheritance and other legal rights of women can be found in the court battles, for example, between Dolley Madison and the brother of her late first husband, Julia Tyler and her brother over their late mother's property, Mary Lincoln's insanity trial initiated by her son, even Rachel Jackson's divorce from her first husband, Lewis Robards.

Among First Ladies were several southern women who, at one point in their lives, owned, or whose families or husbands owned slaves: Martha Washington, Martha Jefferson Randolph, Dolley Madison, Elizabeth Monroe, Rachel Jackson, Emily Donelson, Sarah Yorke Jackson, Angelica Van Buren, Letitia Tyler, Julia Tyler, Sarah Polk, Margaret Taylor, Mary Lincoln, Eliza Johnson, Julia Grant, Ellen Arthur and Edith Wilson. Many of their attitudes towards slavery was simply acceptance of it as a way of agrarian life.

Few are known to have expressed moral outrage at it. "Mr. Polk, the writers of the Declaration of Independence were mistaken when they affirmed that all men are created equal," Sarah Polk told her husband while watching slaves working on the lawn. "There are those men toiling in the heat of the sun...Those men did not choose such a lot in life, neither did we ask for ours; we were created for these places." [1]

The complex range of emotions from affection to disgust experienced by slave-owning First Ladies is part of the larger and still unexplored area of study about the relationships of plantation women and slavery.

On the other hand, there were several northern First Ladies who were abolitionists, or raised in abolitionist families: Abigail Adams, Louisa Adams, Anna Harrison, Jane Pierce, Abigail Fillmore, Lucy Hayes, and Lucretia Garfield. During the bloody battle that broke out in Kansas following President Pierce's signing of the Kansas-Nebraska Act permitting these new territories the option to vote to permit slavery, the otherwise subdued Jane Pierce felt strong-

Louisa Adams Born, reared and educated in Europe, Louisa Adams recorded bitter thoughts about the intellectual and legal subjugation of women in American society, but it led to her later support of the abolition movement.

Copyright 1903, by Bureau of National Literature & Art.

"General Jackson and his Lady"
Rachel Jackson's life provides a case study of legal rights affecting women in divorce and bigamy in the early 19th century. Before her husband was elected President, his opponents portrayed her as a "wanton" woman. Although it looks nothing like her, she was famous enough to be a subject in a folk art painting with the famous General of the Battle of New Orleans her husband.

ly enough to persuade her husband to free an imprisoned abolitionist accused of treason.

The abolition movement was the first organized effort in which American women formally joined together to fight for a cause. Many of the leaders and principals of the organized abolition movement provided the seeds for later women's public reform efforts. Interestingly, although Mary Todd Lincoln was reared in a family that held and sold slaves in Lexington, her maternal grandmother aided in the Underground Railroad movement to secretly help slaves into free territory. As First Lady, at the pinnacle of civil war, Mrs. Lincoln was a rabid abolitionist and befriended one of the leading women abolitionists at the time, Jane Grey Swisshelm, who attested to her commitment and perhaps even influence on the President, in regard to emancipation. "I recognized Mrs. Lincoln as a loyal, liberty-loving woman, more staunch than even her husband in opposition to the rebellion...she was more radically opposed to slavery...[and] urged him to Emancipation as a matter of right, long before he saw it as a matter of necessity." [2] But Mary Lincoln's own family history and youth, during which she could see the slave trade from a bedroom window, provides the fuller context of a southern woman who evolved to despise slavery.

In counterpoint is the New York born and educated Julia Tyler, who married a southern slave owner and came to believe in slavery. As a former First Lady she even wrote an open letter to England's abolitionist Duchess of Sutherland in 1853 that was published widely throughout America and Europe, defending the "peculiar institution" as a uniquely native problem that hardly required advice from the British government, given their treatment of the Irish. "Spare from the well-fed Negroes...one drop of your superabounding sympathy to pour into that bitter cup [Ireland] which is overrunning with sorrow...relieve many a poor female of England, who is now cold, and shivering...I reason not with you on the subject of our domestic institutions. Such as they are...We prefer to work out our Destiny..." [3] Yet in looking at the baronial lifestyle of her childhood in a family that owned its own island, one can see how a northerner like her could adapt easily to slavery.

The lives of First Ladies both before they entered and after they left the

White House also provide a fuller context for studying women's history. How, for example, did their youthful sensibilities about "women's issues" as young women change once they came onto the national stage and, afterwards, how did that change affect their beliefs and practices as former First Ladies? Louisa Catherine Adams is one of the fascinating figures, for example, in terms of the issue of abolition. Educated in French convents in a sophisticated curriculum, she expressed what might today be termed feminist thought on how a political wife lived like a "prisoner." As she wrote bitterly to her husband, "That sense of inferiority which by nature and by law we are compelled to feel and to which we must submit is worn by us with as much satisfaction as the badge of slavery..." [4] Sympathy was borne in her for any downtrodden American, including the working class maids that served her class. From this came a growing passion and support for the abolition of African-Americans held as slaves, concurrent with her husband's post-presidential career as a Congressman in the 1840s. While her consciousness on the issue came after her White House tenure and thus she neither spoke out or took action as an abolitionist First Lady, a study of her correspondence with figures like the pioneering abolitionist sisters Angelina and Sarah Grimke provides a rich tale of a European woman in America confronting its most heinous chapter.

The creation of the Women's Christian Temperance Union in 1873 brought forth the popular caricature of the prim-faced moralist in black bonnet and spectacles decrying the sins of demon rum and all other alcohol. It was an image personified by the grim visage of Carrie Nation who brandished an axe that she used to smash up saloon bottles. Far less severe were the tens of thousands of American women who joined and supported the organization, believing that a woman was responsible for the sanctity of the family and faith – and that alcohol undermined both. Alcoholism was a rampant problem in American homes in the mid-19th century, and women were the most frequent and direct victims of abuse from alcoholic husbands.

In First Lady history there is an interesting dichotomy of those who personally abstained from alcohol and those who thought it proper to ban the serving of any alcohol to their public guests at the White House. Sarah Polk, in the White House during the religious revival movement of the 1840s, was a strict Calvinist who never drank alcohol and frowned on its use but nevertheless served wines to her dinner guests. Reaction was overwhelmingly positive from the religious press. The famous and controversial ban on alcohol of all kinds under the Hayes Administration was widely attributed to its First Lady, although Lucy Hayes followed the lead of her husband. Still, she became a symbol of the rising and often derided temperance movement and, specifically, the WCTU (which she refused to join but which attached themselves to her nevertheless). Mrs. Hayes's correspondence and the numerous articles written about her provide a glimpse of the increasingly powerful "dry" movement to make alcohol illegal in America. Successors such as Lucretia Garfield, Frances Cleveland, and Nellie Taft were petitioned by the WCTU to pledge to their organization and ban alcohol in the White House – but none cooperated. Refusal by even Lucy Hayes to overtly

Jane Pierce Although she was in every other way a removed and depressed First Lady, when Jane Pierce learned that a fellow abolitionist had been imprisoned for his part in the violence following the President's signing of the Kansas-Nebraska Act – which extended slavery – she insisted on the man being freed. She succeeded.

Photo of young Lucy Webb with two fellow women graduates (top right), **Lucy Webb grade report from Wesleyan College** (top left), **Photo of Frances Folsom with her classmates** (middle left), **Hillary Rodham delivering graduation speech at Wellesley** (bottom left), **Lou Henry in geology classroom at Stanford** (bottom right) Rabid abolitionist Lucy Webb Hayes, the first First Lady to attend college, expressed an early interest in women's rights in a school essay. She formed a close bond with her fellow students at Cincinnati Wesleyan Female College, from which she graduated in 1850. Frances Folsom graduated from Wells College just a year before her 1886 White House wedding to President Cleveland and became a role model for other young American women pursuing higher education. In 1898, Lou Henry became possibly the first women in America to graduate with a degree in geology. It

was while pursuing her degree at Stanford that she met fellow geology student Herbert Hoover. Hillary Rodham, active in student government at Wellesley College, was chosen by the college president to deliver a commencement address. Excerpts of her speech and her photo appeared in *Life Magazine* in 1969. She was the second First Lady to earn a graduate degree, Pat Nixon was the first.

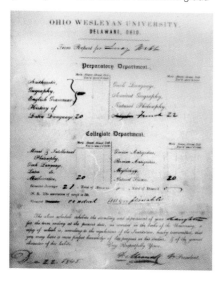

involve herself in temperance or women's education left some women activists quite frustrated. Journalist Emily Briggs wrote Mrs. Hayes that American women should be told whether she favored "the progress of women in the high road of civilization or whether you are content because destiny lifted you to an exalted position, so high and far away that you cannot hear the groans of the countless of our sex..." [5]

One area of women's history to which First Ladies history provides a more thoroughly chronicled evolution is women's education. A handfull of small schools and academies created specifically for the education of women were already established, mostly in New England and New York, when Abigail Adams was First Lady. Yet even since before the American Revolution, she had been philosophically debating her husband on the need for equal access to education by the female gender. Her writing on the subject, indeed her changing views on gender equality, is well documented from the 1770s to the 1810s. In terms of the young nation's evolving concepts on women's education, Abigail Adams provides a good record to study since she made frequent comment and observation on the subject. Those among the First Ladies who came from wealthy families – and they are the majority – offer a unique opportunity for analysis of the changing curriculum taught to young women in what were considered some of regional America's best private women's schools and colleges of the 19th and early 20th centuries: Madame Greland's Seminary in Philadelphia, Miss Graham's in New York City, Madame N.D. Chagaray's Institute in New York City, Moravian Academy in North Carolina, Georgetown Visitation Academy in Washington, Dr. Ward's co-educational school in Lexington, Kentucky, Rhea Academy in Nashville, Houghton Seminary in New York State, Brooke Hall in Pennsylvania, Miss Nourse School in Cincinnati and Barstow School in Kansas City.

Much was made in the press about the fact that Lucy Hayes had attended and graduated from Wesleyan Women's College, making her the first First Lady to graduate from college. By coincidence, the immediately succeeding presidential wives also earned college degrees – Lucretia Garfield from Eclectic Institute, Frances Cleveland from Wells College, Caroline Harrison from Oxford Female Institute (later became part of Miami University). At a time when the very issue of equal access to higher education for women was being debated in American society at large, the lives of the First Ladies spoke as a definitive statement on their view. The arguments against higher education for women had often been based in the perception that it would train women for their own careers and

Caroline Harrison and DAR Caroline Harrison, a former teacher, was an older woman who had youthful notions on equality for women. Seen here seated in the center, with founding members of the Daughters of the American Revolution, she served as the heraldic and professional women's organization's first president-general.

Young Nellie Taft with two women friends A lifelong lover of beer, a cigarette smoker, and adept at poker, young feminist Nellie Herron (far left) – after giving up her dream of being a writer – went to work as a teacher so she could earn her own salary and not depend on her father or a prospective husband. She would not accept William Howard Taft's offer of marriage until she felt that he respected her intelligence.

thus somehow erode the foundation of society by removing masses of women from motherhood and household duties. Although she herself did not graduate from college because of limited family finances, First Lady Nellie Taft addressed the issue head-on, in defending her daughter Helen's pursuit of a college education and an academic career. "I believe in the best and most thorough education for everyone, men and women...Education for women, as much as is obtainable, possesses to my mind, far greater advantages than the commercial one of providing means for making a livelihood. This is a very great benefit, when necessary..." [6]

Women's education became an issue closely associated with and supported by First Ladies. Florence Harding made a point of inviting classes of girls' schools to the White House as reward for graduation. When the popular Grace Coolidge – a graduate of the University of Vermont – became the first First Lady to receive honorary degrees, she was held up as a "college girl" model for young women in the 1920s, even in a *New York Times* editorial. Her warmth and intelligence, the article ran, "could hardly have been possible without the contribution of college, which is happily now for women." [7] As a former First Lady, Frances Cleveland worked to help create the first woman's college in the New Jersey state system. By the time Lou Hoover came to the White House as the first woman to graduate with a degree in geology, from Stanford, erudition and high academic achievement for women found their greatest role models.

The course of college study and professional directions taken by later First Ladies also provide a profile of 20th century American women of different socioeconomic and regional backgrounds who earned college degrees and worked before and (in fewer cases) after marriage: Grace Coolidge, a University of Vermont graduate who went on to teach deaf students; Jacqueline Kennedy, a French literature major at George Washington University who became a reporter; Pat Nixon, a graduate of the University of Southern California who became a teacher; Nancy Reagan, who studied drama at Smith College and became an actress; Hillary Clinton, who earned her bachelor's at Wellesley, then her law degree at Yale and became an attorney; and Laura Bush who earned her bachelor's at Southern Methodist College and became a teacher, then earned her graduate degree in library sciences from the University of Texas at Austin and became a librarian. Others who earned academic degrees later worked in fields outside of their study – Rosalynn Carter served as the business manager of her husband's agricultural industries and Lady Bird Johnson became manager of a radio station. Those searching for fuller academic records of the course of study followed by women in different eras may also find a more substantial record of this in the papers of First Ladies; unlike their unknown contemporaries, the school records of numerous First Ladies were preserved as part of the larger efforts to document their lives.

Numerous First Ladies worked and earned their own salaries because of financial necessity within their families, to support themselves as they lived on their own or simply to learn a trade: Abigail Fillmore as a teacher, Eliza Johnson as a quilt-maker and shoemaker, Lucretia Garfield as a teacher,

Caroline Harrison as a music teacher, Ida McKinley as a bank clerk, Nellie Taft as a kindergarten and boy's school teacher, Edith Wilson as a jewelry store owner, Florence Harding as a piano teacher and newspaper business manager, Pat Nixon as a bank teller, cleaning woman, model, acting extra, teacher and economist, Betty Ford as a department store buyer and canned food factory worker, Rosalynn Carter as a hairdresser, and Hillary Clinton as a child hospital aide, frozen fish factory worker and law school teacher. Regardless of the class of these women, all evidence suggests that their exposure to a world beyond their own, widened their perspectives and understanding in a manner that enhanced their empathy as First Ladies.

Many First Ladies had the passion of altruism and, or the luxury of wealth that permitted them to work as volunteers in a variety of capacities during their lifetimes. These were largely in traditionally female spheres such as nursing, teaching and secretarial work. Abigail Adams was the first such First Lady to assume a public duty outside the home when she was appointed, with two other women, by the Massachusetts colony's General Court to question Tory women. "You are now a politician," her husband wrote her, "and now elected into an important office, that of judges of the Tory ladies, which will give you, naturally, an influence with your sex..." [8]

Abigail Adams had famously admonished her husband to "remember the ladies" while he served in the Second Continental Congress at the time of the Declaration of Independence's drafting. In numerous letters she argued the case to her husband that women should be given full civic rights by the government of the new nation. The organized fight for women's suffrage, began at the 1848 Seneca Falls Convention, was led by Lucretia Mott and Elizabeth Cady Stanton. Sixteen Presidential Administrations presided over by First Ladies from Sarah Polk to Edith Wilson passed until the end of the struggle in 1920 when national suffrage became law with the 19th Amendment.

For twenty years, Presidents and their wives rarely took the idea of women's suffrage seriously. Slavery of African-Americans remained the primary issue of concern. In 1869, however, Elizabeth Cady Stanton and Susan B. Anthony created the National Women's Suffrage Association and began organized lobbying and protest efforts to give women the vote. In 1878, Susan B. Anthony drafted a simple constitutional amendment calling for suffrage, and a California Senator introduced it. It would be repeatedly introduced in each new congress to allow it to be brought to the Senete and House floors for at least a full debate until it passed in 1919. First Ladies consistently voiced their opposition to suffrage. Mary Arthur McElroy and Frances Cleveland even

Edith Wilson As a poor young girl from the hills of Virginia, Edith Bolling married an older, wealthy man who died after eight years of marriage, leaving her a wealthy widow and owner of his family jewelry and silver shop. After marrying the widower President as her second husband, she thought that the women who picketed the White House for the right to vote were "disgusting creatures."

Eleanor Roosevelt with women reporters In the depths of the Great Depression, Eleanor Roosevelt helped keep the women of the Washington press corps from being fired by editors who – in cutting costs – thought they were the most dispensible: she initiated weekly press conferences in the Green Room of the White House for women reporters "only."

joined anti-suffrage organizations. Mary Lincoln and Edith Wilson found the outspoken character of women suffragists to be the objectionable element. The former suggested that if given the vote, "our strong minded sisters" would "behave in so inconsequent a manner as to reduce the whole matter to an absurdity." [9] This was a prevailing argument used by both men and women who opposed suffrage.

In some instances such a view may also have been a reflection of their husbands' official opposition to the amendment; there is some suggestion of sympathy if not full support. In earlier life, Lucy Hayes and Lucretia Garfield wrote essays supporting it. Ellen Wilson privately supported suffrage but would not admit that to the press since her husband opposed it. As a former First Lady, Julia Grant came to support the cause once it was carefully explained to her – and because of a personal friendship with Susan B. Anthony. During her husband's 1908 candidacy for the presidency, Nellie Taft finally broke precedent and told a reporter that she supported suffrage – as long as women were not run as candidates. Finally, when the 19th amendment seemed to be a foregone conclusion, just awaiting state ratification during the 1920 election, Florence Harding vigorously declared, "Yes, I'm a suffragist," and later spoke openly about her belief. "The time has passed for discussion about the desirability of having the women actively participate in politics. They are in politics, and it is their duty to make their participation effective, and of real service to their country. This necessarily means that much and aggressive effort is needed to maintain their interest, and to inform them concerning issues and public problems." [10]

The post-World War II push for equal civil rights of women at the executive level, culminating in the organized effort to create a Constitutional amendment known as the Equal Rights Amendment, was first introduced in 1923 by Republican Senator Charles Curtis of Kansas. None of the three Republican First Ladies of the 1920s offered their view of it, and Eleanor Roosevelt opposed it for many years fearing, as many women's groups did, that it might undo decades of protective legislation for women. Only at the end of her life did she suggest her support for an ERA, during her chairing of President Kennedy's 1962 Commission on the Status of Women. The former First Lady's writings and speeches as commission chair provide an inside glimpse on the development of their findings and recommendations.

Interestingly, Jackie Kennedy took no especial interest in the commission at the time. Yet if one looks at her life after the White House, one sees an evolution that many middle-class suburban wives and mothers of the Fifties and Sixties went through. In tracing her remarks and writings once she returned to work full-time as a publishing editor in 1975, as well as consideration of her close friendship with feminist leader Gloria Steinem, a sort of case study in Jacqueline Kennedy Onassis unfolds. While it may specifically be the story of a rich and famous celebrity going to work, it is curiously representative of many more average women who earned college educations, briefly pursed careers, then married and raised children for decades, only to return to work once the children were grown: "What has been sad for many women of my generation is that they weren't supposed to work if they had families." [11]

Republican First Lady Pat Nixon was the first First Lady to offer her verbal support of the ERA, but it was a major effort of her successor and fellow Republican Betty Ford. In perhaps her most remarkable of speeches, at the Cleveland International Year of the Woman Congress, Mrs. Ford declared, "Many barriers continue to block the paths of most women...the limits on women have been formalized into law...the first important steps have been to undo these laws that hem women in and lock them out of the mainstream of opportunities...I do not believe that being First Lady should prevent me from expressing my views..." [12] As First Lady she lobbied governors and other state legislators to, at the very least, permit the ERA to be brought to a vote in the statehouses for ratification.

In 1976, when former California governor Ronald Reagan challenged

Florence Harding's Daughter of the Nile silver membership tag (top), **Florence Harding with women tennis players** (middle), **Florence Harding with college sorority women on front steps of White House** (bottom) First to declare herself "a suffragist," first to vote for her husband for President, first to fly in an airplane, the only one to declare that she did not wear a wedding ring, Florence Harding was also the first openly feminist First Lady. She promoted the idea of women involving themselves in politics, seeking economic education and parity, and even foresaw a day when women were the family breadwinners. She belonged to a wide variety of women's clubs, from the American League of Pen Women to the Daughters of the Nile (as her silver membership card above attests to), hosted a woman's tennis match on the White House lawn, and welcomed groups of college girls to receptions.

President Ford for the Republican nomination, one of the schisms that developed in the party was based on the debate of whether the party should support or abandon the ERA. That same year, for example, former Republican First Lady Mamie Eisenhower expressed many of her generation's bewilderment at the very idea of ERA. "I don't know about this Ms. business....I never knew what a woman would want to be liberated from." [13]

Rosalynn Carter took up Betty Ford's support of the ERA and the two of them, along with Lady Bird Johnson, also attended the Houston National Women's Conference. Nancy Reagan, as a candidate's wife in 1976 and then, as the nominee's wife in 1980, made clear her belief

Jackie Bouvier as young reporter (top), **Lady Bird Johnson** (bottom) Before marrying Jackie Bouvier and her successor Lady Bird Taylor both briefly pursued careers in journalism after graduation from college.

that existing laws were already in place to provide equal rights for women and that a constitutional amendment was unnecessary and unwise. Mrs. Reagan's view even provoked feminist writer Betty Friedan to speak out publicly on her dismay with her fellow Smith College classmate's views on equal rights.

Although as a future First Lady Barbara Bush was on the record as being pro-ERA during her husband's failed 1980 campaign for the Republican presidential nomination, she and most of her party resisted pushing for it once it failed to win the last three necessary state ratifications, after an extension to 1982. Interestingly, as a former First Lady Betty Ford continued her push for the ERA, attending the 1980 Republican convention with the intention of headlining a pro-ERA Republican parade in Detroit, the host city. She later wrote that she deeply regretted being talked out of it as she watched the women in white parading from her hotel window. Later, she joined former First Lady Lady Bird Johnson at a mass 1982 Washington rally at the Lincoln Memorial supporting in a last-ditch, failed effort to enact ERA passage.

Even more controversial than her support of ERA was Betty Ford's outspoken support of the Supreme Court decision in Roe vs. Wade, striking down anti-abortion laws and upholding the right of women's reproductive choices. Decided in 1973, it was actually Pat Nixon who first expressed her support of the decision, but Mrs. Ford's comments – in combination with her addressing numerous other social issues – made headlines. At varying times before, during or after their White House tenure, Jacqueline Kennedy, Rosalynn Carter, Nancy Reagan, Barbara Bush, Hillary Clinton and Laura Bush all voiced their support of the decision. As early as the 1920s, however, issues of reproductive rights had been raised with First Ladies, when Florence Harding refused to publicly condemn Margaret Sanger's crusade for birth control.

A history of women's health issues is told within the most private stories of some First Ladies, whether it be the gruesomely rudimentary and modestly performed details of the surgery Louisa Adams underwent, the expectation to remove oneself from society if one showed visible signs of physical weakness that Nellie Taft adhered to after her stroke, or the news blackout initiated by the President's press secretary concerning the delicate subject of Mamie Eisenhower's 1956 hysterectomy.

It was again Betty Ford who was a pioneer in both First Lady and women's history when, in September 1974, she permitted the White House to fully divulge details of her breast cancer and surgery. Medical experts at the time credited her as saving perhaps untold tens of thousands of women's lives. She was the first public figure to so openly address a health issue that had long been taboo for public discussion. Nancy Reagan's personal decision to have a full mastectomy when she was struck with the illness further stirred public debate on the choices available to women at the time in defeating the cancer. Hillary Clinton took a large interest in a variety of women's health issues and successfully pushed for the Medicare coverage of mammograms. Laura Bush, whose mother had also had breast cancer, continued to discuss the issue. As a former First Lady, Betty Ford raised national consciousness of the unique reasons and ensuing problems faced by women who suffered from alcoholism and drug addiction, after publicly disclosing that she herself was beginning recovery for the dual diseases.

Discussion of health problems unique to women were often considered too delicate a subject for polite conversation in the 19th and much of the 20th century, although medical books and journals were available for consultation in private. Not until the end of the 19th century, for example, did a First Lady support the idea of women being trained as doctors to serve other women, when Caroline Harrison helped raise funds for Johns Hopkins Medical School with the understanding that it would admit women students. Edith Roosevelt and Nellie Taft were among the first of several First Ladies to help raise interest and funds for the local Columbia Hospital for Women and its free clinic providing health care to low-income pregnant women.

In the mid-19th century, an attitude that equated femininity with submissiveness prevailed, and several of the physically and emotionally weaker First Ladies, like Elizabeth Monroe, Louisa Adams, Margaret Taylor, Jane Pierce, and Mary Lincoln seemed the very embodiment of such an attitude. By the end of the 19th century, however, women of the elite class were beginning to participate in gentle sporting activities like lawn tennis and golf. Several First Ladies who had been teenagers at that time came to the White House as middle-aged women who nevertheless continued to maintain their health with regular exercise and regiments: Edith Roosevelt rode daily on her horse in local parks and streets, Nellie Taft took brisk daily constitutions, Florence Harding enjoying fishing, Grace Coolidge swam and played tennis, both Lou Hoover and Eleanor Roosevelt hiked and rode horses, and the latter even learned to dive into pools. Several of these women also became public proponents of what some of the older generation still considered unfeminine behavior – competitive sports for girls and young women. Florence Harding advocated that the Campfire Girls assume a full range of "open air life and healthful games" as a way of strengthening them for the larger roles they would be playing outside the home. [14] She also hosted a woman's tennis tournament at the White House. No First Lady was more active in promoting physical strength and exercise for women than Lou Hoover. The only woman vice president of the National Amateur Athletic Federation, she also founded its women division. While often seen as a traditionalist, Lou Hoover's views on the equality of women in all fields physical and professional show her to be one of the most thorough feminists among First Ladies.

Most of the First Ladies were hesitant to address controversial issues. They were more comfortable discussing or having information disseminated on them in what was their most familiar context – as wives and mothers. Studying the lives of First Ladies as part of the history of family and marriage is also a window on evolving American perceptions of these institutions. Examining how and what they taught their sons and daughters reflects not only their own values but those of society at large. Specific training and educational principles on childrearing were recorded as early as Abigail Adams

MISS COOPER as HELENA.

Priscilla Cooper as actress in theater poster (above), **Nancy Davis as actress in movie still** (opposite right) In 1841, after marrying the son of Vice President John Tyler, who succeeded to the presidency in just one month after Harrison's death, the former stage actress Priscilla Cooper married a president's son and served as First Lady for her paralyzed mother-in-law. A poster advertises her performance as Desdamona in *Othello*. Exactly 140 years later, another former actress became First Lady. After graduating from Smith College and working as a volunteer nurse and a department store saleswoman, Nancy Davis performed on stage, television and screen before her 1953 marriage to fellow actor Ronald Reagan, as seen in a publicity photograph.

and as recently as Jackie Kennedy, who famously remarked, "If you bungle raising your children I don't think whatever else you do well matters very much." In later years, she added an afterthought about having been a young mother while serving as First Lady: "And why shouldn't that be an example, too?" [15]

Their marital roles illustrate the economic, social and political development, aid and support they gave their husbands on the climb to the presidency. Yet whether they were in conflict or continuity with the prevailing notions of an ideal American wife, studying the roles they assumed in their relationships provides unique case studies of the history of marriage. There is rich material to be mined in this sphere, whether it be a highly unusual 18th century American marriage like, for example, the partnership of John and Abigail Adams or an utterly predictable one a hundred years later like that of Calvin and Grace Coolidge.

For most of presidential history, First Ladies, like all women were defined by the men in their life – father, husband, brother and son. (Even in more recent times this was often a charge against First Ladies, as when a

group of Wellesley students voiced their objection to having Barbara Bush deliver their commencement speech because her "identity" was through her husband, or when Hillary Clinton decided to support rather than spurn her husband in the personal scandal that led to his impeachment.) Woman was expected to reign and rule in her separate sphere of the home and her success was measured in terms of faith and morality, childrearing, and domestic management. As the middle class rose in the wake of the Industrial Revolution, women had more "idle" time and many more now hired inexpensive labor to do the domestic chores (which the women were still responsible for managing). It was in that spare time, in their "ladies parlors" and, increasingly outside of it, that women who were financially supported began to expand their interests in the worlds outside the home – the neighborhood, the civic community and the nation. It is in this context that American women's history and First Ladies history has perhaps the fullest story to tell.

In the early 19th century, local charities drew upon the largesse and support of prominent society women. Thus, when asked, Dolley Madison helped to establish the Washington Orphans Asylum for Girls. Considering her prominence in local life, however, Mrs. Madison was an exception. Most

other First Ladies limited their charity efforts to their adopted churches in Washington. As far as being solicited to join national organizations, prior to the Civil War, there is no indication that the patronage of First Ladies was sought. Margaret Taylor, for example, was awarded life membership in the Sunday School Union because she was simply with the President at the ceremony where he was inducted. Harriet Lane, first exposed to organized social reform drives while in England during her uncle's service as Ambassador to the Court of St. James, sought to improve the lot of several Native American tribes, but it was not an organized effort. When Mary Lincoln began making donations to and purchases for the Contraband Relief Society (to provide sanitary shelter, food and clothing for freed slaves) and soliciting wealthy friends to also do so, it was the first time a First Lady aligned herself with an organization. She had done so at the suggestion of her seamstress Elizabeth Keckley, a former slave.

Often organized through church or community groups, the movement for social reform pre-dated the Civil War, but the creation and membership of such organizations by women intensified afterwards: The General Federation of Women's Clubs was founded in 1892, for example, and the American Home Economics Association in 1908. When the Daughters of

Ellen Wilson painting (opposite), **Ellen Wilson with examples of her paintings behind her** (right) Known as "Ellie the man-hater," because of her determination to pursue a professional career as an artist and not get married, Ellen Axson graduated from the New York Art Students League and went on to display in professional exhibitions. She set up a work studio in the White House. The accompanying landscape, "Autumn Landscape," was completed in 1911.

the American Revolution was founded in 1890 more as a patriotic and political women's group than a heraldic one, its first president was no less a person than the First Lady, Caroline Harrison, and she delivered her first speech to the group in the White House: "Since this society has been organized and so much thought and reading directed to the early struggles of this country, it has been made plain that much of its success was due to…women of that era. The unselfish part they acted constantly commands itself to our admiration and example. If there is no abatement in this element of success in our ranks, I feel sure that their daughters can perpetuate a society worthy the cause and worthy themselves." [16]

As the DAR sought to teach immigrants about the American heritage, the National Civic Federation sought to uplift the poor by improving their working conditions and housing. Nellie Taft joined and addressed the women's division of the NCF after her husband's election in 1908. Before she suffered a stroke, she had intended to focus on upgrading the workspaces for women employed in government offices. That goal, as well as the initiation of a Congressional bill calling for the demolition of unsanitary alley dwellings near the Capitol, was achieved by her successor Ellen Wilson, also in tandem with the NCF women's division.

World War I called forth hundreds of thousands of women to do their part for the war effort at home and abroad through the American Red Cross – which was largely run by women. Among the few wartime appearances without the President made by Edith Wilson (who otherwise showed no interest at all in women's issues) were Red Cross efforts. Many of her successors would lend their support to the Red Cross in the ensuing decades. Although disabled military men

returning from World War were the national constituency most closely associated with Florence Harding, she was an avid supporter of numerous women's reform organizations, professional associations and clubs, and frequently welcomed large groups of them en masse to the White House. Mrs. Harding was herself a member of numerous clubs – the DAR, the National Pen Women, the National Women's Press Association, the Daughters of the Nile, to name but a few.

Grace Coolidge continued the custom of inviting women's groups to the White House, such as the Visiting Nurses Association, but it was purely ceremonial. Certainly no First Lady was more directly linked to supporting various women's organizations than Eleanor Roosevelt; her efforts on behalf of a vast diversity of women was so wide that it is more accurately stated that the "advancement of women" was one of her primary focuses, rather than her ties to any one woman's organization. Her genuine commitment to reform reached back to her own settlement work among the poor immi-

Jackie Kennedy's painting of angel sold as Christmas card (top), **Caroline Harrison's painting of orchids used as product giveaway** (middle) Although two First Ladies – Caroline Harrison and Jackie Kennedy – who were skilled artists in various media including oils, watercolors, drawing, and pottery, did not pursue professional careers in art, they did permit their original work to be used commercially. Copies of Caroline Harrison's orchid painting were given away as a promotional for a women's magazine. Jackie Kennedy's angel painting, and one of the Three Wise Men, were sold in boxes to raise funds for a National Cultural Center in Washington, D.C.

grants of New York as a member of the Junior League and continued into her later married years when she worked closely with other women consumer protection and labor union advocates.

Eleanor Roosevelt's immediate successors Bess Truman and Mamie Eisenhower closely reflected the "club woman" of the Atomic Era and 1950s, more associated with homemaking or leisure activities like gardening and bridge clubs. In the latter part of her tenure, however, Mamie Eisenhower led a national effort of the American Heart Association that called forth all women to collect donations door-to-door for heart research. Certainly in more contemporary times there is no greater illustration of a First Lady's close relationship with professional women seeking to improve various aspects of American life than Lady Bird Johnson. While her "Beautification" efforts were greatly aided across the nation by hundreds of women's garden and civic clubs, it was her frequent "Women Doer Luncheons" that drew national women experts from various organizations together. After a White House lunch and lecture on one of the many social ills of the 1960s, the group would debate tangible solutions to the issue under discussion.

Perhaps the most dramatic example of a First Lady's direct role in the development of what remains the largest girl's organization in America is Lou

Eliza Johnson (top), **Caroline Harrison funeral ribbons** (middle), **Betty Ford in hospital bed** (bottom) Women's health issues have been dealt with in the White House as it was in every house in America. Eliza Johnson was the classic "retiring, kind, gentle, old lady, too much of an invalid" – as Julia Grant recalled her. Although her chronic tuberculosis kept her confined to her bedroom suite, the door to her sitting room was always kept open – so she could keep an eye on who was meeting with the President in his office across the hall. Although Letitia Tyler was the first incumbent First Lady to die, it was the death of Caroline Harrison from tuberculosis in the midst of her husband's re-election campaign that stunned the nation into mourning. A ribbon from her funeral wreathes was pulled and preserved by the President. Betty Ford's full 1974 disclosure that she had breast cancer not only broke a social taboo of openly discussing the widespread and potentially fatal disease, but shocked thousands of women into seeking their first check-ups for it.

Henry Hoover. Although founder Juliette Gordon Low is most closely associated with the Girl Scouts of America, Lou Hoover's pre-White House stint
as the GSA president resulted in a national organization magazine, substantial fundraising for camping programs and leadership training. Infusing a
democratic system giving freedom to different troops to decide what they
wished to focus on, as First Lady she also put the GSA to a unique use.
During the Great Depression, she sought to create a national voluntary relief
program of a quarter of a million Girl Scouts to serve the needs and requests
for food and other necessities in local communities. Lou Hoover steadfastly
believed in the power of organized women's groups and later devoted herself to the League of Women Voters as well as the GSA. In reference to the
former organization, she declared, "As a strictly nonpartisan organization the
League can be and will be more of a power behind the throne... We need
women as well as men in politics. To make a party whole there should be as
many feminine as masculine minds." [17]

While some women turned outward into the community, others took
the equally self-actualizing opportunity to pursue their own talents and self-
development in reading and writing, painting and other artistic endeavors
that helped to develop independent voices for women. Louisa Adams wrote
copious amounts of poetry and several plays, focusing on the plight of
women in society. Nellie Taft found an outlet for her love of music by founding and serving as the president of the Cincinnati Symphony Orchestra, and
later became the first to write and publish her memoirs. Her successor, Ellen
Wilson, was well known as an artist in her own right, a graduate of the New
York Art Students League who had her own professional show before entering the White House. As First Lady Caroline Harrison continued her pursuit
of china design and watercolors, and her artistic skills were so publicized
that one of her flower paintings was widely reproduced for the public.

Despite the increased leisure time for women of wealth, other societal
expectations arose. For example, although intended to reduce the workload
of the kitchen, the creation of mass-manufactured
cooking utensils actually anticipated larger and
more complicated entertaining duties of middle-
and upper-class women. From this was borne
magazines and books providing ideas and guid-
ance for women. The first and most prominent of
these was the *Godey's Ladies Book* magazine, the
first issue of which appeared in 1837 (it had been
in publication as the *Ladies Magazine* since 1828).
With the literacy rate among American women
increased to 50 percent by 1850, such magazines
and books guiding women to conform on everything from dress code to manners only became
more popular. *Ladies Home Journal* began publication in 1883, *Good Housekeeping* in 1885 and
Vogue in 1893.

By the late 19th century, First Ladies were

Lou Hoover riding horse (opposite top right), Eleanor Roosevelt learning how to dive at poolside (opposite bottom right), Rosalynn Carter jogging (top right), Barbara Bush biking (bottom) An adamant public advocate for women's athletics, Lou Hoover stirred some controversy by suggesting that women were equal to many of the physical sports that men played. She is seen here on her daily ride. Although a swimmer since childhood, Eleanor Roosevelt had long hesitated to dive, but was delighted at overcoming her fear after a staff member trained her. She is seen here practicing poolside in Hyde Park. In the late 1970s, like many other Americans Rosalynn Carter began pursuing a healthy lifestyle of eating and exercise and often jogged with family members around Washington. Despite her image as a white-haired grandmother, Barbara Bush maintained her physically active lifestyle – biking, playing tennis and swimming.

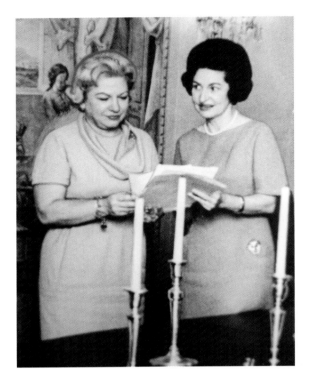

Mamie Eisenhower with mother, daughter-in-law, grand-daughter, and Ike (opposite top right), **Jackie Kennedy Onassis with Gloria Steinem** (opposite middle left), **Lady Bird Johnson and Liz Carpenter** (opposite top left), **Pat Nixon doing yoga** (opposite bottom), **Betty Ford wearing ERA button** (top), **Barbara Bush with Raisa Gorbachev at Wellesley College** (bottom) The original idea of "feminism," as in a woman's choice to pursue the direction of her own life, was also employed by those First Ladies whose primary roles were traditional. Living in a highly matriarchal family, President Eisenhower is seen here with his granddaughter, wife, mother-in-law and daughter-in-law. Mamie Eisenhower insisted on taking responsibility for her husband's salary, maintaining their expenditure records, keeping their finances balanced, and doling out an allowance to him. Although her mother and husband had discouraged her pursuit of a professional writing career, Jackie Kennedy managed to help draft, illustrate and edit her first book while she was First Lady, the historic guide to the White House. Thirteen years later, she went to work as an editor. She is seen here with her friend Gloria Steinem, feminist writer, activist and magazine editor. Lady Bird Johnson is the only First Lady who hired a professional newspaper journalist as a press secretary, her friend Liz Carpenter. A leader in the women's movement who bridged the traditional and progressive generations, Carpenter helped Lady Bird Johnson address feminist issues in a modulated manner. A former schoolteacher, movie extra, model and economist, Pat Nixon was the first First Lady to publicly declare her support for the Equal Rights Amendment, appointing a woman to the Supreme Court and the Roe vs. Wade ruling. She is seen here practicing diaphragmatic breathing during yoga. As the very model of the suburban Middle American mom, Betty Ford vigorously championed the ERA by appealing to housewives and women bankers, lobbying governors and state senators and doing press interviews. Delivering the 1990 Wellesley commencement – and bringing Soviet First Lady Raisa Gorbachev along – Barbara Bush implored graduates to "learn about and respect difference" including the choices that women make in their lives. She added that a future presidential spouse might be in the audience that day, "And I wish him well."

regularly featured in such magazines, held up as the idealized hostess in the nation's number one home, portrayed as keeping America's hearth on an even keel. In this regard, the notion of the First Lady as a role model housekeeper, hostess, manager of servants, gardener, cook, decorator and fashion model was conveyed to the masses of women. Just how close to reality the "first housekeeper" or "first hostess" really was to the average women who read about them, would make an interesting comparative study. While many women may have copied Jackie Kennedy's chocolate mousse recipe or Edith Roosevelt's decorating style, for example, neither of those First Ladies would have known the dessert's ingredients or how to cut and sew curtains. On the other hand, women of working- and middle-class origins like Lucretia Garfield, Caroline Harrison, Grace Coolidge, Bess Truman, Pat Nixon, Betty Ford, Rosalynn Carter, Hillary Clinton or Laura Bush certainly might.

It was women who most frequently wrote about First Ladies for the general public in popular women's magazines and newspaper articles. Unique relationships thus arose among several First Ladies and women writers and journalists. The earliest example of this was the blurry line that was continually crossed by Margaret Bayard Smith, the wife of a national newspaper editor, and Dolley Madison. Often socializing together, they served each others' purposes: Mrs. Smith got an exclusive insider view of Mrs. Madison's life while Mrs. Madison got good press as a result of it. Margaret Smith even used Dolley Madison as the heroine character in her novel, *What is Gentility?* When Smith asked Mrs. Madison for cooperation in writing the first biographical sketch of her, the First Lady flatteringly responded that, "your pen would be more agreeable to me than any other..." [18]

Mary Clemmer Ames was the first woman journalist who regularly covered the First Lady as her "beat," and it was through her columns that much of the national praise for Lucy Hayes was generated. Florence Harding believed strongly that women were ideally suited for journalism, and she held

Picture of Florence Harding in Girl Scout uniform (top left), **Florence Harding Girl Scout uniform** (top right), **Grace Coolidge wearing uniform with Girl Scout officials** (opposite bottom), **Lou Hoover speaking to Girl Scout leaders** (opposite top) Founded by Juliette Gordon Low during the Wilson Administration because the Boy Scouts would not consider a girl's branch, the Girl Scouts of America initially threatened those who feared it would promote the idea that girls should take on what boys were trained to do: be physically active and fit, volunteer in public, learn self-reliance and endure the rigors of outdoor life. Although an inactive Edith Wilson accepted honorary presidency of the organization, her three immediate successors were instrumental in helping establish its respectability. As National President of the Girl Scouts from 1922 to 1925, Lou Hoover believed the organization would only succeed if adult women served as role models. At the same time, Mrs. Hoover – seen here with troop leaders – was also a Cabinet Wife during the tenures of Florence Harding (whose uniform appears above) and Grace Coolidge – both of whom vigorously promoted the organization and wore their adult uniforms to organization meetings. As First Lady, Mrs. Hoover made national radio addresses to the organization.

informal press conferences for them and encouraged the individual career of at least one reporter, Jane Dixon, by providing exclusive interviews to her.

On a larger and more dramatic scale, Eleanor Roosevelt helped to permanently establish women reporters in the Washington press corps by holding weekly, formal press conferences. Many of Eleanor Roosevelt's innovations as First Lady may, in fact, have resulted from advice and suggestions provided to her by Association Press reporter Lenora Hickok and *New York Times* reporter Bess Furman, both of whom became personal friends. Similarly, Lady Bird Johnson, through her press secretary Liz Carpenter – a former reporter herself – cultivated friendships with women reporters, such as Isabel Shelton, Helen Thomas, Fran Lewine and Betty Beale. Carpenter, an activist on behalf of gender equality in her own right, recognized that the roles of women were changing in the 1960s; while the reporters had covered traditional aspects of the First Lady's life such as entertaining, they were also now encouraged to cover substantive issues in which Mrs. Johnson was involved. In many respects, the changing role of newspaperwomen in the 1960s and 1970s was boosted by the activities of Lady Bird Johnson. In the 1980s, *Washington Post* columnist and reporter Donnie Radcliffe closely covered the daily activities of Nancy Reagan – whether it be the First Lady's clothing or her political involvement behind the scenes. By the time Hillary Clinton was First Lady, reporters covering her had to be as

familiar with contemporary art as it did universal health care proposals.

Even less explored than the relationship between First Ladies and women reporters is that between First Ladies and women elected to, or actively involved in politics. Dolley Madison was generations ahead of many of her successors in her belief that not only she, but also other women should be informed of the political process, despite not being able to vote. She often took women with her to the visitor's gallery at the Capitol to take in political debates and speeches. There are also numerous examples of First Ladies who sought to place women into government positions – from Caroline Harrison who successfully suggested the President's woman stenographer, to Betty Ford and Hillary Clinton who urged the appointment of women Cabinet members.

The 1872 press portrayed, and the public viewed the first woman to declare herself a candidate for the presidency, Victoria Woodhull, as largely a humorous oddity. Still, many women who did support suffrage hesitated at the idea of a woman filling political positions. Nellie Taft, for example, voiced the view that having women actively seek and serve in political office would upset the balance of the home by taking her away from the responsibilities of the domestic sphere. Florence Harding firmly spoke out in favor of women becoming politically active, congratulated women elected to Congress and suggested that as more women rose in the ranks and experience within the parties they would be elected to higher positions. Although she supported a project of the National Women's Party honoring suffragette history, she believed that women should not form their own party but rather enlist in the two established parties. She also sought to bring women political figures to meet with her husband. "I want to help the women of the country to understand their government and their duty to their government," she explained to a reporter, "I want representative women to meet their Chief Executive and to understand the policies of the present administration." [19]

Eleanor Roosevelt, herself active in New York politics and national democratic party politics a decade before she became First Lady, assiduously sought to enlist women in the Democratic party and worked closely with the national party's women's division chief Molly Dewson to do so. Mrs. Roosevelt also reached out to women elected or appointed to political position to coordinate mutual efforts, and believed firmly that women were equal in all aspects to men in politics. She became the first First Lady to actively promote the candidacy of a woman candidate for Congress, her friend Caroline O'Day. As a former First Lady and chair of the Commission on the Status of Women, she urged President Kennedy to name more women to government posts. As a Vice President's wife and later as First Lady, Pat Nixon frequently called for women to learn more about the political process and work for their parties. She voiced her disappointment that a much larger number of women – commensurate with the actual population - were not elected to Congress and was the first First Lady who sought to have a woman named to the Supreme Court. "Our population is more than fifty percent women, so why not? A woman will help to balance the Court." [20] Although she admitted that the title of the newly formed Women's National Political Caucus "sounds pretty wild," she supported their goal of electing more women to Congress "even if they were not Republican. I've always believed in supporting the person, not the party." [21]

Hillary Clinton in Africa speaking to women During her numerous trips to eastern Europe, Asia, the Middle East and Africa, Hillary Clinton met with women's groups seeking legal freedoms for medical, educational, social and economic equity.

Photo courtesy of The White House

Laura Bush meeting with Afghanistan women As Americans freed Afghanistan from the radical Taliban regime, which forbid by death the education, medical care and professional pursuits of women, Laura Bush held a 2001 meeting with exiled Afghani women eager to rebuild women's lives in that nation.

By the time Laura Bush was in the White House, numerous First Ladies had specifically campaigned for the election of women to the House and Senate. The popularity of Hillary Clinton among women Democrats made her an influential figure with them, and she was a frequent speaker on behalf of women candidates at the state and national level. Her 2000 election to the United States Senate – the first First Lady ever elected to her own political position – certainly inaugurated a new era in the unique combination of women's history and First Lady history.

Further research into the lives and activities of the First Ladies will undoubtedly turn up more evidence of their interest or views on issues affecting the women of their times: protective legislation, women's unions, anti-pornography and anti-prostitution campaigns, volunteer war work, anti-war efforts, widowhood, divorce, financial independence, professional women's organizations. However much it might seem that a First Lady is remote to the harder realities and controversial issues faced by the masses of American women, parallels and shared experiences can be discovered within the personal experiences of the full lives of these four dozen women.

[1] Anson and Fanny Nelson, *Memorials of Sarah Childress Polk* (New York: Anson D.F. Randolph & Co., 1892) p. 99

[2] Anthony, p. 188

[3] the letter of Mrs. Tyler to the Duchess of Sutherland appeared in numerous publications, but first in the January 28, 1853 issue of the *Richmond Enquirer*

[4] Anthony 109-110

[5] Emily Apt Geer, *First Lady: The Life of Lucy Webb Hayes* (Kent, Ohio: Kent State University Press, 1984), p. 169

[6] quoted in Edna Colman, *White House Gossip* (New York: Doubleday, 1926) p. 324

[7] *New York Times*, March 28, 1927

[8] Anthony, p. 32

[9] Anthony, p. 246

[10] Florence Harding to Anna Churchill Moulton Tillinghast, November 21, 1921, Warren Harding Papers, Ohio Historical Society

[11] Gloria Steinem, "Jacqueline Kennedy Onassis Talks About Working," *Ms. Magazine*, March 1979

[12] Pullen Papers, Box 3, October 25, 1975 speech of Betty Ford to International Year of the Woman Cleveland Congress, Gerald R. Ford Presidential Library

[13] Nick Thimmesch, "Mamie Eisenhower at 80," *McCall's*, October 1976 and *Buffalo Evening News*, November 13, 1979

[14] "Mrs. Harding Wants Organization to Equal that of Boy Scouts," *Philadelphia Public Ledger* clipping no date (circa April 1923) Florence Harding scrapbooks Harding Papers, OHS, and Florence Harding to Love Chapman, president of the Campfire Girls, *Washington Star*, November 4, 1921

[15] Jacqueline Onassis to author, December 8, 1989, quoted in Anthony, volume 2, p. 46

[16] Special Collections Pertaining to the history of the National Society of the Daughters of the American Revolution, Caroline Scott Harrison Collection, box 7, folder 23

[17] quoted in Helen Benton Pryor, *Lou Henry Hoover: Gallant First Lady*, (New York: Dodd, Mead, 1969) p. 130

[18] Anthony, p. 83

[19] Abby Gunn Baker, "With the Hardings in the White House", *Christian Herald*, August 27, 1921

[20] *Ladies Home Journal*, February 1972]

[21] ABC-TV Virginia Sherwood interview with Pat Nixon, 1971, Nixon Archives Project, National Archives

"...POLITICS AND INTRICACIES..."

Presidential and Political History and First Ladies by Carl Sferrazza Anthony, Author and Historian

I had always had the satisfaction of knowing almost

as much as he about politics and intricacies of any situation

in which he found himself.

-Nellie Taft

In the American Presidency, specifically, and national politics, generally, there has always been what Nancy Reagan humorously termed the issue of "the boss's wife."

In widely diverse methods, the First Ladies have impacted the political and governmental processes: direct participation in legislation and policy; working alliances with other political figures; personnel; campaigning; and most importantly, personal influence over the President. First Ladies have contributed to presidential history in both large and small ways. History has proven, too, that the First Lady is the wild card in politics: the potential for her power over the President and, ultimately, political decisions can be great and remain an unknown factor. For, despite all the detailed examples that are known of First Ladies' political roles and involvement in the presidencies of their husbands, much more remains speculative, undocumented and so secretly conducted as to be lost to history.

The most overt and obvious form of political influence of First Ladies occurs when they step out publicly on behalf of legislation or policy initiatives of their husbands' administrations. When the proposed legislation is specifically related to an issue that they are expert on, or which they personally believe is important, it makes their effort all the more political, for the President will often make his staff feel an especial duty to seeing the First Lady's bills through to success. Recent presidential history provides more visible and tangible evidence of this. With her expertise as a teacher and librarian, Laura Bush testified on January 24, 2002, before the Senate Committee on Health, Education, Labor and Pensions, speaking on early childhood development and education. Mrs. Bush's testimony before Congress marked the fourth time in history that an incumbent First Lady did so; Eleanor Roosevelt first did so before the House District of Columbia Committee in 1945, reporting on conditions in local institutions such as schools, retirement houses, and homes for indigent children; Rosalynn Carter testified on mental health before the Senate Subcommittee on Health and Scientific Research of the Human Resources Committee in 1979; and Hillary Clinton testified in 1993 on behalf of health care reform before a House committee on the administration's health care plan. In the 1990s, as former First Ladies, Betty Ford, Rosalynn Carter and Nancy Reagan have also testified, the former two, jointly, on mental health and drug use, and the latter on Alzheimer's.

Certainly none was so overtly involved politically that she helped to achieve more federal legislation than any other First Lady than Hillary

Eleanor Roosevelt at Office of Civilian Defense job Eleanor Roosevelt worked as the unsalaried co-director of the Office of Civilian Defense, walking to her office from the White House everyday. Attacks from Congress prompted her resignation.

(on the left top to bottom) **Caroline and Benjamin Harrison at his desk, Eleanor Roosevelt with coal miners, Lady Bird Johnson in Head Start classroom.** (opposite top to bottom) **Rosalynn Carter presiding over Mental Health Commission, Hillary Clinton at State Union Address in Capitol** Numerous First Ladies helped foster and or lobby on behalf of federal legislation. Caroline Harrison, peeking over the President's desk, won a partial victory in getting Congressional funds to renovate the White House. Eleanor Roosevelt got federal funding and helped plan and oversee "Arthurdale," an experimental housing development for coal mining families in West Virginia (she is seen here famously descending into a mine). Lady Bird Johnson helped in the creation of the Head Start war on poverty Program, and is seen here in a session of it in a school. Rosalynn Carter oversaw sub-committees, traveled the nation and interviewed experts in her role as Honorary Chair of the President's Commission on Mental Health, resulting in new Executive Departments policy and Congressional passage of the 1980 Mental Health Systems Act. Hillary Clinton, descending Capitol steps to hear her husband's State of the Union Address, that same year helped craft and lobby for the Safe Families Act of 1997, helping children into better adoption and foster care. Mary Regula is seated in the front row second from the right.

Clinton. While she was most widely associated with the Health Care Reform Act which failed to pass in Congress, her continuing work on health issues, as well as banking, education, and equal rights concerns is less well-known. During her eight-year tenure, Mrs. Clinton fostered numerous domestic reforms including a 1997 bill which helped expedite the adoption process, increased research funding for a variety of health issues ranging from epilepsy to prostate cancer, creation of health insurance coverage for children in families unable to provide it for them, and micro-loans for new, small businesses, to name but a few. On the international level, she also worked in tandem with the International Monetary Fund in initiating small businesses in many underdeveloped nations, championed the movement for a civil society in newly created democratic nations in Eastern Europe, and actively sought to involve the women of various nations in their own government's political processes through the Vital Voices foundation, which she helped to found.

Rosalynn Carter was also overtly involved in legislation, most notably the Mental Health Systems Act of 1980, which sought to streamline mental health community services. She worked closely with members of the Cabinet and Congress for three years in shaping the legislation, after chairing a presidential commission on mental health. Mrs. Carter's role in a presidential commission raised an issue from the past and for the future. Conflict of interest law now prohibited a federal official like a president to employ a close relative such as a spouse. Even though Mrs. Carter was not going to be salaried, she had to take the title of "honorary" of the commission. Similarly, Eleanor Roosevelt had faced constant Congressional and media criticism when she became the unsalaried co-director of the Office of Civilian Defense, during the time of war-preparedness and ultimately had to resign her position.

With no salary or official title, Hillary Clinton's heading of the Clinton Administration's Health Care Reform Task Force in 1993 raised an issue that, unwittingly, gave more formal status to the role of First Lady within the federal government. So-called sunshine laws stated that any presidential commissions or task forces that had non-officials as active participants had to hold all of its meetings and make all of its paperwork open to the media and public. The White House Counsel's office successfully made the case in court that a First Lady is officially a federal government figure. One of the strongest bits of evidence favoring this decision was based on Public Law 95-570, which passed in 1978 when Rosalynn Carter was First Lady. That law provides federal funding for the staff of a presidential spouse in as formal a job description as "First Lady" gets: "Assistance and services...are authorized to be provided to the spouse of the president in connection with assistance provided by such spouse to the president in the discharge of the president's duties and responsibilities."

Mrs. Carter also sought to see the passage of the Equal Rights Amendment, continuing the national efforts of her predecessor Betty Ford. Although Mrs. Ford had not been involved in the shaping of the ERA's language – the proposed amendment having long before been crafted – she

Nancy Reagan and Ronald Reagan preparing for joint television interview (opposite top), **Nancy Reagan with children at "Just Say No" rally at White House** (opposite bottom), **Nancy Reagan watching Ronald Reagan sign 1986 Anti-Drug Abuse Act** (above) A First Lady need not draft legislation to bring policy into public discourse. Although Nancy Reagan's anti-drug abuse program was intended to educate children through "Just Say No" clubs in their schools, it dovetailed with Administration initiatives. She became its most visible spokesperson on the subject, making a joint television address to the nation with the President on the subject, the first First Lady to do so, and was publicly at his side when he signed the 1986 Anti-Drug Abuse Act.

Cartoon of Frances Cleveland carrying her husband in chair on her back (opposite top left), **Cartoon of Julia Tyler** (opposite bottom left), **Cartoon of Florence Harding and Warren as "President and Mr. Harding"** (opposite bottom right), **Cartoon of Jackie Kennedy on "Mount Ruskmore"** (bottom right), **Cartoon of Betty Ford as "Betty Ross" for Bicentennial year ERA effort** (top right) Editorial cartoons of First Ladies tying them to politics first appeared in 1844, when the image of a parasol-carrying Julia Gardiner Tyler seemed to be leading John Tyler into retirement and away from running for re-election that year. Frances Cleveland is seen in the next one, her popularity so great that it could carry the political attacks that weighted down the President in his last term. Florence Harding and her husband were identified with a string of 1920s celebrities as "the President and Mr. Harding." Jackie Kennedy's personal diplomacy with British Prime Minister Macmillan, French President DeGaulle, Moroccan King Hassan, and Indian Premier Nehru smoothed State Department negotiations with their nations. Betty Ford's ERA support coincided with the Bicentennial era's reflection on women's Revolutionary War roles.

Betsy Ford—1975

became its most prominent proponent, speaking across the country for its passage, lobbying governors and other state officials, and raising the issue in her many media interviews. Similarly, Florence Harding did not initiate the legislation providing for the first all-women's federal penitentiary, but she spoke to reporters about her lobbying efforts on its behalf with the House Speaker. She also helped prompt the federal property expansion of Zion National Park in Utah.

Lady Bird Johnson was the first First Lady who fostered federal legislation on an issue affecting the land of the entire nation with her 1965 Highway Beautification Bill, which sought to erase the presence of billboards, junkyards and other eyesores along national highways. There was substantial resistance to passage of the bill, largely by congressmen who represented small districts where local businesses depended heavily on billboard advertising. "I love that woman and she wants that Highway Beautification Act," President Johnson barked to his staff and legislative aides, "By God, we're going to get it for her." [1]

Prior to this effort, several other First Ladies were involved in federal legislation that focused on conditions in Washington, D.C. As earlier cited, Eleanor Roosevelt testified before Congress on behalf of her inspection and report of deplorable conditions in local institutions. Extending back a generation, several of her predecessors were also behind efforts that involved improvements in the District of Columbia. Ellen Wilson initiated the Alley Dwelling Clearance Act of 1914, well-intended though somewhat misguided legislation to clear out the slums around the capital city where the poorest residents lived in horrific conditions – but with no provision to provide new housing for the displaced. Nellie Taft, in her efforts to redevelop West Potomac Park as a public space for band concerts and site for her planting of the famous cherry blossom trees, worked through her husband to successfully seek a $25,000 Congressional appropriation.

Other First Ladies – not generally viewed as "political" were in fact formidable proponents of federal legislation or funding in connection with renovation, restoration or expansion plans of the White House. Since the mansion was as much a private residence as a public institution, their efforts were easily presented as simply those of concerned chatelaines of the house, clearly within a traditional domestic role. Thus they escaped any potential censure for involving themselves in policy. In this way, Jacqueline Kennedy initiated what would become Public Law 87286 after lobbying Senate Interior and Insular Affairs Committee chairman, New Mexico Senator Clinton Anderson. The law established the White House as an historic site, with the various protective measures necessary into securing its preservation. Grace Coolidge was able to solicit gifts and funds for restoration by an act of Congress. Caroline Harrison won a partial victory in her bid to expand the mansion by receiving substantial renovation and cleaning funds of $35,000. Abigail Fillmore secured Congressional funds to create the mansion's first permanent library.

Still other First Ladies quietly supported and took an avid interest in passage of legislation that related to their chosen causes, but without any

Elizabeth Monroe silhouette (opposite top), **Letitia Tyler** (opposite bottom), **Margaret Taylor** (above) As attested to by their husbands and other government officials, even First Ladies who were in poor health, and relied on their daughters to serve as hostesses, provided support and advice that furthered their husbands' political fortunes. Examples include Elizabeth Monroe, Letitia Tyler and Margaret "Peggy" Taylor, the last pictured in a photograph from a private collection.

publicity or testimony before Congress: Barbara Bush and the National Literacy Act, Nancy Reagan and the Anti-Drug Abuse Act, Pat Nixon and the Domestic Volunteer Services Act, and Jacqueline Kennedy and the creation of the National Cultural Center and a presidential commission on the arts and humanities. To what degree these women and others were involved in the legislation is not always clear. "I don't get into anything in front of Congress," Barbara Bush declared, for example, in regard to suggestions that she testify before Congress on the National Literacy Act, which called for local libraries to be used as literacy learning centers and the recruiting of a "literacy corps" through VISTA, the national voluntary organization. In recent years, however, Barbara Bush stated that she was particularly proud of the bill. At the time she decided against supporting it publicly, one of the act's sponsors, Illinois Senator Bill Simon told the *Washington Post* that he was certain the First Lady would be a "secret lobbyist" for it. He may have been right. [2]

Far more First Ladies have had a private influence on policy or other government related decisions. Most of these examples have been in minor matters, although Abigail Adams vigorously pushing the case for the Alien & Sedition Acts and Eleanor Roosevelt fostering the creation of the Federal Emergency Relief Administration's and Civil Works Administration's women divisions, National Youth Administration, Works Progress Administration, Federal Writers Project, Federal Theater Project and Federal Art Project are important exceptions. Mary Lincoln – evidently with her husband's permission – recommended military supply merchandisers to Union Army quartermasters. Bess Truman convinced her husband to increase National Institute of Health research funding for cancer and to approve a State Department cultural exchange program. Florence Harding halted the Commerce Department's commissioner of fisheries from permitting the killing of seals for the sake of fishing.

In an example of what can be termed a negative influence, Edith Wilson made no effort to present the full reality to her sick and bedridden husband of the strong resistance to his plan for American entry into the League of Nations and she furthermore refused to strongly press the case for compromise. At a time when her power over him was at its peak, many historians believe that Edith Wilson could have helped pave the way for passage of a moderated version of the League, her influence over the President's thinking being great – but she did not.

Still other examples of First Ladies' influences on government are based on legend and lore suggesting, for example, that Dolley Madison successfully lobbied to keep the capital city in Washington, D.C. after its government buildings had been burned during the War of 1812, rather than returning it to Philadelphia, or that Abigail Fillmore influenced her husband to ban flogging in the navy or that Eliza Johnson urged her husband to craft a lenient Reconstruction policy towards the defeated South. Any paper trails on these and other claims of First Lady's influences on the government process have yet to materialize.

Evidences of another form of influence – intercessions on behalf of citizens who appealed to First Ladies – are more plentiful. Thus, there is proof that Dolley Madison helped to free a conscientious objector from prison during the War of 1812, Julia Tyler managed to commute the death sentence of "Babe," a notorious New York pirate, Nellie Taft introduced the President to an African-American teacher who sought and thus received his support to open a school for poor black children in the deep South, Florence Harding helped a persecuted Jewish man to immigrate to the United States out of Russia. Starting with the presidential library system's archival preservation of First Ladies' papers, the record of women from Lou Hoover to Hillary Clinton and how they responded to such requests is abundant.

Despite the fact that prevailing 19th century concepts of women's proper roles in society did not in any way encourage them to participate in politics, in the highest circles of political power around a President, the opinions and inquiries of a First Lady received due respect from members of the Cabinet, Senate, House, Supreme Court and Governors. In numerous instances, First Ladies created their own independent alliances with such men, often serving as a bridge of support or information to their husbands. Dolley Madison, for example, cultivated a friendship with the powerful bloc of young congressmen from the western states and territory, led by Kentucky's Henry Clay. Known as the "War Hawks" their support was crucial in Madison's re-election as president in 1812. The First Lady and Congressmen even shared pinches of snuff together. The young, attractive

Mamie Eisenhower hugging President at airport (above), Eisenhower watches Mamie lifting arms in victory presidential podium (bottom) When the President suffered a 1954 heart attack, Mamie Eisenhower took charge of his hospital sickroom, his staff respecting her privilege to do so. She monitored his sleep, work, nutrition and health for the rest of his Administration, even secretly limiting his speaking commitments in the 1960 election. He later revealed that he sought her opinions on everything from West Wing personnel to an economic theory he learned at a conference.

and flirtatious Julia Tyler used her winsome manner to lobby Congressional leaders and even Supreme Court Justice McLean for support of the President's proposal for a joint resolution on the annexation of Texas. Harriet Lane, who was the official hostess of our only bachelor President James Buchanan, had close social relationships with the southern members of her uncle's Cabinet; when several of them began to fall away as talk of secession began, it was she who went to them, trying to keep them within the fold by drawing on the loyalty of friendship. When her husband was out of Washington, Sarah Polk frequently spoke with members of her husband's Cabinet during the Mexican War, reporting back her impressions to the President. "I saw Mr. Buchanan last evening," she wrote in wartime about the Secretary of State to the President when he was away from the White House, "he was full of foreign news, but I learned nothing very specific." [3]

Other First Ladies drew upon their earlier associations with political figures: Edith Roosevelt served as a secret liaison between old friend Cecil Spring-Rice, now a diplomat, when he had confidential information to convey to the President; Nancy Reagan's trust and history of friendship with Senator Paul Laxalt served her well when he ran the President's re-election campaign and she felt that it was not functioning well during the debates, as did her longtime closeness to Presidential advisor Mike Deaver throughout Reagan's first term on numerous political matters; Jackie Kennedy's comfort level of showing her own political acumen with men she had known prior to her husband's election – advisors Arthur Schlesinger and Dick Goodwin, U.S Ambassador to India John Kenneth Galbraith and Assistant Defense Secretary Roswell Gilpatric, Senator Claiborne Pell to name several – allowed her to consult them for advice and to solicit their views on how to best achieve some of the legislation she wanted the President to initiate with Congress.

Other examples include First Ladies who only came to know political figures during their husbands' presidencies, but with whom a mutual admiration served the purposes of accomplishing the women's own goals in projects. Examples of these include Caroline Harrison and California Senator Leland Stanford – with whom she allied to get her petition to fund the extension of the White House passed in the Senate, and Ellen Wilson and Postmaster General Albert Burleson and Treasury Secretary William McAdoo, both of whom followed through on their promise to her to provide better working conditions in their departments.

Such relationships became more frequent in the latter 20th century as First Ladies pursued passage of legislation in areas related to their own special projects. In her environmental restoration efforts – dubbed "beautification" – Lady Bird Johnson developed a close working relationship and friendship with Interior Secretary Stewart Udall. When Rosalynn Carter was diligently trying to keep her mental health legislation a priority amid growing crises in 1979 and 1980, she often turned for help to Health, Education and Welfare Secretary Joseph Califano and House Speaker Tip O'Neill. She already had a good working relationship with Congressmen Claude Pepper in her efforts on behalf of senior citizens.

Edith and Woodrow Wilson standing together at ballgame
Edith Wilson began offering the President unsolicited advice while they were courting. During the war, she learned his secret code and after his stroke she assumed what she would only term "stewardship" of the presidency.

Florence Harding and Eleanor Roosevelt, both of whom openly rec-commended policy changes and initiatives, worked closely with Cabinet members who, while dutifully reporting to the First Ladies when they made requests, were also comfortable enough with them to disagree upon occasion: the former had such relations with Attorney General Harry Daugherty, Navy Secretary Edwin Denby, and Commerce Secretary Herbert Hoover; the latter with Labor Secretary Frances Perkins, Treasury Secretary Henry Morganthau and Postmaster General Jim Farley. When Eleanor Roosevelt initiated an experimental housing and community project in West Virginia known as Arthurdale, the First Lady beset Interior Secretary Harold Ickes with endless requests and complaints. He wished she would "stick to her knitting and keep out of the affairs connected with my department." When she refused, he eventually resigned because "a constant repetition of these groundless charges on her part is found to have an effect...on the President." [4]

Considering how fully involved Hillary Clinton was in Clinton Administration policy, it is hardly unusual that she would have maintained professional relationships with the President's chiefs of staff Mack McLarty, Leon Pannetta, Erskine Bowles and John Podesta and members of his Cabinet, most notably Secretary of State Madeleine Albright, Health and Human Services Secretary Donna Shalala, Treasury Secretary Robert Rubin and Attorney General Janet Reno. Since she was also intricately involved in helping to draft and foster various pieces of legislation, the First Lady held meetings or conferred by phone with members of Congress from both parties in efforts to shepard such initiatives to passage. More recently, Laura Bush has reportedly shared her husband's personal friendships with Presidential Advisor Karen Hughes and Condoleezza Rice of the National Security Council.

Even those friendships that First Ladies developed with political figures that were not based on any pending legislation or pressing issue could also ultimately serve the political purposes of Presidents. Mary Lincoln's friendship with Massachusetts Senator Charles Sumner was based, initially, on their mutual love of opera and literature. As they went out together and became even closer, Mrs. Lincoln often brought the rabid abolitionist home for informal and relaxed conversations with the President, certainly making the Senator a closer ally of the Administration. When Lucretia Garfield urged her husband to appoint James G. Blaine as Secretary of State despite a skeleton in his past, he developed a rabid loyalty to the President, although he was otherwise known as a wily and self-interested politician.

Certainly there is no more dramatic an example of

Calvin and Grace Coolidge in mourning for their son Shy to the point of becoming anxious with strangers, Calvin Coolidge had depended heavily on his wife's extroverted personality and engaging social skills to aid the necessary public relations of politics. He became deeply depressed after his teenage son's sudden death; Perhaps the greatest role Grace Coolidge played was, she said, her effort to "teach him to enjoy life," although he wasn't "very easy to instruct in that way."

"She Was Able to Reveal to Him the Mystery of Books."

Eliza Johnson advising Andrew Johnson during the impeachment trial   Hot-tempered to begin with, Andrew Johnson's impeachment trial created tremendous anxiety for him. Eliza Johnson not only kept him emotionally calmed, but also constantly reassured him that he would be acquitted. He was. In his early years, it was she who encouraged his entrance into local politics and helped him prepare speeches and strategy.

just how great an impact a First Lady can have as a result of her alliance with political figures than the saga of Edith Wilson's self-described "stewardship" during her husband's October 1919 stroke and the weeks and months immediately afterwards. Mrs. Wilson interpreted Secretary of State Robert Lansing's decision to hold a Cabinet meeting without the President as absolute disloyalty and successfully engineered his ouster and replacement with Bainbridge Colby. Colby was so grateful that as Secretary of State, he was a complete toady to the First Lady. Numerous officials were complicit in her cover-up of the true nature of Wilson's illness and followed instructions from her – which she claimed were from the President – never questioning the validity of such an ad-hoc process.

Mrs. Wilson successfully expelled unofficial presidential advisor and friend Colonel Edmund House from the President's inner circle, marginalized the influence of the President's devoted press secretary Joseph Tumulty, and refused to have the credentials of the new British Ambassador Lord Gray accepted - because of a personal slight made to her by his attaché. This all occurred during the crucial time Wilson's League of Nations was before the Senate and played a part in its demise. Pre-dating this, however, Mrs. Wilson also made the argument with the President – both before and after their 1915 marriage – that his first Secretary of State William Jennings Bryan was not serving the best interests of the Administration and should be let go. Interestingly, the first Mrs. Wilson, Ellen Axson, had been a proponent for Bryan's appointment. There are no other instances that compare with Edith Wilson's extensive power in the hiring and firing of personnel and staff, but there are numerous other examples both documented and alleged.

While there are no specifics regarding which Cabinet members or other officials whose appointments that Abigail Adams may have aided, in her voluminous correspondence there are frequent references to her professional judgments on the abilities of numerous public figures. When the President appointed a member of the opposition party, one William Vans Murray, to help negotiate with the French – with whom Adams had barely avoided a war – he wrote to his wife of the reaction in the press. "Oh how they lament Mrs. Adams' absence! She is a good counselor! If she had been here, Murray would never have been named nor his mission instituted!" [5] Even those wives who were not known to involve themselves in any aspect of the presidency seemed to weigh in on personnel, sometimes for the most personal reasons. Margaret Taylor, for example, successfully urged the appointment of prominent Maryland lawyer Reverdy Johnson as her husband's Attorney General simply because he was a relative of hers.

Part of the reason why much speculation still exists about the role of First Ladies in personnel is that it dramatically raises the issue of whether this should be a prerogative of a presidential spouse. Not only does this sort of influence potentially stunt or damage the public careers of accomplished individual but the veto or dismissal of such an individual can be based as much on personal chemistry of a First Lady and the person in question as much as (or even rather than) professional qualification and policy considerations. Edith Wilson's earlier stated vendetta against Lord Grey is a prime example. Nellie Taft also permitted personal resentments to guide her influence on the President's candidates for ambassadorships. She halted the imminent appointment of former President Theodore Roosevelt's son-in-law, Congressman Nicolas Longworth as U.S. Ambassador to China because of her dislike of him and his wife. Her lingering resentment towards U.S. Ambassador to England Henry White (dating to her honeymoon in England when, as an embassy staff member he did not get her tickets to take in Parliament) is believed to have been a factor in his not being kept in that position. She was also a factor in having the President's private secretary (the equivalent of the modern-day Chief of Staff) Fred Carpenter removed from the West Wing and sent to Morocco as U.S. Ambassador, because she judged him to be too weak with Congress.

Due to the sensitive nature of this sort of influence, many suggestions of First Ladies' roles in personnel remain unconfirmed until the time that their papers are opened to researchers. Even appointments that resulted in positive results are not always quickly credited to the wisdom of First Ladies. Barbara Bush, for example, was strongly rumored to favor her husband's appointments of Louis Sullivan and Jack Kemp as Secretaries of Health and Human Services and Housing and Urban Development, respectively, though she never remarked on this in her memoirs.

Another factor which makes a First Lady's influence on personnel more prevalent is that it is honestly viewed by both Presidents and their wives as simply an outgrowth of marital support, the idea that one spouse should seek to help the other in their business by reporting on those associates they view or know to be attributes or liabilities. As Nancy Reagan said in numerous interviews, her questioning the judgments of individuals such as National Security Council members Dick Allen and William P. Clark, advisors Ed Meese and Jim Baker, and Chief of Staff Don Regan, was not getting into "policy" but rather "people issues." She watched carefully for those who might "end-run" the President. In this specific arena of influence, even First Ladies considered the most apolitical carried weight. "She is a very shrewd observer," former President Dwight Eisenhower admitted of his wife Mamie, "I frequently asked her impression of someone, and found her intuition good. Women who know the same individual as a man do give a different slant...I got it into my head that I'd better listen when she talked about someone brought in close to me." [6]

In many of the known cases where First Ladies' advice on personnel has been followed, the results have generally benefited the Administration - Bess Truman's push for the

John Adams greeting Abigail Adams as she exits coach
Parodied in the press as "the Happy Old Couple," President John Adams made no apologies for relying heavily on the advice and input of his intellectual wife Abigail. "I think you shine as a Stateswoman," he wrote her. More virulently anti-French than he was, the President nevertheless ignored her advice to engage the young nation in war with France.

Photograph of Sarah Polk (top), James Polk locket – campaign picture (bottom) Without the traditional duties of motherhood, Sarah Polk devoted her life to her husband's political career, advising him on issues of the day like the federal banking system. She served as his personal assistant, marking newspaper articles and editorials that she felt were important. She wore this locket with the image of her husband, taken from a campaign print.

appointment of *St. Louis Post-Dispatch* editor Charlie Ross as the President's Press Secretary, Betty Ford urging that Carla Hills be made Housing and Urban Development Secretary and Eleanor Roosevelt convincing her husband to name Harry Hopkins as head of the National Relief Administration. This has not been true in every case. Florence Harding was a particularly bad judge of bad character, notably in her urging the appointment of Veterans Bureau administrator Charles Forbes, whose criminal activities in that post led to widespread scandal and his eventual imprisonment.

Nor should it be assumed that a First Lady's advice always holds sway. Julia Grant advised her husband on a number of occasions to rid himself of close friends who had been placed into political positions whose intents she mistrusted. "Ulys, how can you let a man like that stay in your Cabinet?" she had questioned the President on Postmaster General Marshall Jewell a full year before Grant finally dismissed Jewell. She similarly expressed her mistrust of the Interior Secretary and Attorney General, her judgment proving correct in both instances. [7] One of Grant's closest friends and advisors Adam Badeau later remarked that, "the president would not overthrow a man whom he trusted though there were occasions when it would have been better for him had she [Mrs. Grant] succeeded." [8] Nor should it be assumed that a First Lady's ignored advice results negatively. While Lincoln was aware that his wife's harsh assessments of men like Secretary of State Seward, Treasury Secretary Salmon Chase and Union General Ulysses S. Grant were valid, he wisely ignored her suggestions to fire them.

Many First Ladies were recipients of endless pleas for the once-political patronage appointments of post masterships throughout the nation's numerous postal districts and many sought to meet these requests. Julia Tyler even insisted that a cousin of hers – any cousin – be named postmaster of Sag Harbor, Long Island where many members of her family lived. The majority of confirmed reports of First Ladies influencing personnel have been on behalf of minor positions like this: Mary Lincoln papered War Secretary Edwin Stanton with endless requests to appoint soldiers and others to clerical positions in his department; Caroline Harrison saw to it that a friend, Alice Sanger, was named as the first woman stenographer in the executive offices; Dolley Madison had a War Department bookkeeper promoted to head accountant. Before there were laws banning the hiring of close relatives to federal positions, numerous First Ladies encouraged open nepotism as a way of financially helping family members: Abigail Adams, Julia Tyler, Abigail Fillmore, Julia Grant, Nellie Taft and Edith Wilson are among those who helped secure federally-salaried positions for family members.

Certainly the largest – and most carefully guarded – sphere of First Ladies' influence on the political process is the realm of advice and counsel they have provided on issues and problems facing Presidents, particularly during trouble and crises. This is the most provacative role they can play - when the facts are leaked , especially to the public. It inevitably provokes the question, in one form or another, of "Who elected her?" Thus it is usually only with the passage of time, when correspondence collections are opened to researchers and published or when a President or First Lady go on the record themselves that accounts of such influence are definitively confirmed. Even women who publicly voiced their opinions on controversial topics and political issues such as Eleanor Roosevelt and Hillary Clinton did not always disclose the full extent of their advisory roles in the presidencies of their husbands on matters, for example, such as the Japanese bombing on Pearl Harbor or the 1998 impeachment trial, respectively. Two centuries earlier, Abigail Adams felt comfortable enough to openly debate issues with her husband's political opponents like Jefferson. Yet she was shocked when she learned that her views had been quoted at a New England town meeting and even more horrified at the idea of having her revealing political letters published.

Although they did not identify any specific examples of the advice provided them, numerous Presidents and their advisors attested to the wisdom of First Ladies' advice and their sharing the burdens of public life. This is true even in the case of some of the most obscure of First Ladies; in fact, in the absence of any of their own correspondence, it is the word of the President or other political figures that remains as the only documentation of the sagacity of these women. James Monroe called his wife "the partner of all the toils and cares…exposed in public trusts abroad and at home…" [9] Of his first wife, Letitia, John Tyler told his daughter, that he "rarely failed to consult her judgment in the midst of difficulties and troubles, and that she invariably led [me] to the best conclusion." [10] To Senator Jefferson Davis, Zachary Taylor reflected that his wife "Peggy," "was as much of a soldier as I was," and the senator's wife recalled that among the privileged political figures invited to the private quarters where she held court, Mrs. Taylor "took every opportunity to drop a good word in company that might help her husband," and that at dinners she was usually "capably sharing in her part of the conversation." [11]

In other cases, those within their private and advisory circles have credited First Ladies with providing sound advice to their husbands: that Grace Coolidge influenced her husband not to run in 1928 or that Jacqueline Kennedy told her husband he must not trust Khrushchev or any of his Politburo except for Andre Gromyko or, more recently, according to *Washington Post* reporter Bob Woodward, that Laura Bush suggested that her husband be particularly careful in the words he used in rhetorical reaction in the period following the September 11, 2001 attack on America. That such advice was suggested does not mean it was always taken, however wise it might have been to do so, in retrospect. Abigail Fillmore, for example, urged her husband to veto the Fugitive Slave Bill or risk his political career. He ignored her and she proved correct. Pat Nixon suggested that her husband burn his tape-recorded phone calls and conversations while they were still legally considered private property, and to also face individual charges rather than resign and accept a blanket indictment of all charges made against him.

Only in several more recent Administrations is there confirmation through indisputable documentation of specific examples of First Ladies

Abraham and Mary Lincoln reviewing troops in front of White House Involving herself even in military matters during the Civil War, Mary Lincoln reviews troops with her husband and son. She warned him to "distrust" any "ambitious politician," and he quipped, "If I listened to you I should soon be without a Cabinet."

Will and Nellie Taft together on porch "With the troubles of selecting a Cabinet and the difficulties in respect to the revision of the tariff, I feel just a bit like a fish out of water. However, as my wife is the politician she will be able to meet all of these issues," William Howard Taft remarked of his ambitious and savvy wife Nellie just weeks before his 1909 Inaugural.

providing advice on crucial matters. In the case of Lady Bird Johnson, for example, her memos to LBJ outlining her practical reasons that he stand for election in 1964 and then to not do so in 1968, as well as a statement she drafted for him to use at the 1964 Democratic Convention in case the threatened walk-out by the Mississippi delegation occurred in reaction to the seating of African-American delegates (it did not) have been released. In her memoirs, Rosalynn Carter was quite forthcoming in her advice about the Iranian Hostage Crisis. Similarly, Nancy Reagan divulged her own advice to President Reagan that he should begin a personal dialogue with Soviet President Mikhail Gorbachev in the effort to reduce nuclear arsenals. Perhaps one of the more startling acknowledgements of a First Lady's power came from a President. In 1962, when Marianne Means asked former President Harry Truman if he sought his wife's advice even during his decision to drop the atomic bomb, he unequivocally said he had. [12] As for Mrs. Truman herself, she famously destroyed evidence of her playing just such a role. When the President saw her burning some of her old letters to him, he tried to stop her by yelling, "Think of history!" She thrust the rest of the papers into the fire and replied, "I am."

Short of a congressional investigation being held in the presidential boudoir, there will never be a way to fully assess the emotional balance between spouses who live in the White House. In many ways, a First Lady's power is simply a plain fact of the marriage as defined by her and her husband. However, with the pressures and dramatic events that can occur in

Harry and Bess Truman reading in rockers on the Truman Balcony Reading together on the famous balcony he had constructed over the White House South Portico, Harry Truman said of his wife Bess, "She never made a suggestion that wasn't for the welfare and benefit of the country…[on her] counsel and judgment I frequently called. She was a chief advisor and full partner in all transactions – politically and otherwise."

the presidency, there are endless examples of the marital dynamic changing and a President trusting and relying upon his spouse more than any other advisor or aide.

The most well known examples of this have involved situations where a President's health has been in jeopardy: to ensure her husband's healing from surgery in 1986, Nancy Reagan prevented his being scheduled to deliver a State of the Union Address in early 1987 before she thought he was strong enough to endure it; when James Madison fell deathly ill in the midst of the War of 1812, Dolley Madison put off congressional delegates clamoring to meet with him until he was recovered; in 1960, after Eisenhower had suffered through a heart attack, ileitis and stroke, Mamie Eisenhower circumvented his being scheduled to campaign for his Vice President's run for the presidency; Frances Cleveland was fully complicit in the 1893 public deception following her husband's mouth cancer surgery. Throughout the worsening Vietnam War of his five-year presidency, Lyndon Johnson increasingly cut down on his hours of sleep and began to eat irregularly. Lady Bird Johnson focused especially on this, doing all she could to ensure him the necessary rest and nourishment so his health would not worsen.

Nancy Reagan once said that a president has many people to look after various aspects of his political life, but nobody except a spouse watches out for his personal life. Both Reagans were unapologetic about their close emotional relationship and inter-dependency upon each other, even if political decisions and issues were drawn into that relationship. Reagan openly acknowledged his need for his wife's support: "I value her opinion and we talk over everything….I'm not sure a man could be a good president without a wife who is willing to express her opinions with frankness…" [13]

Likewise, a man as different from him as his immediate predecessor, Jimmy Carter, felt the same way about his wife: "There's very seldom a decision that I make that I don't first discuss with her…If I had to bear the responsibilities of a President without her it would be much more difficult for me." [14]

The most private moments between President and First Lady are rarely record-

Richard and Pat Nixon arm in arm Pat Nixon was a sharp critic, active advisor and political partner to her husband while he was Congressman, Senator and Vice President; As President, however, he retreated into a circle of advisors. Her advice to destroy his taped conversations while they were still legally private property and then to not resign and accept a blanket indictment for all the articles of impeachment brought against him was ignored.

Jimmy and Rosalynn having lunch meeting outdoors
"There's very seldom a decision that I make that I don't first discuss with her, very frequently to tell her my options and seek her advice," Jimmy Carter said of his wife Rosalynn, seen here at their weekly lunch meeting. "She's got superb political judgment."

ed. However, it is known that during some of the most intensely trying moments of various presidencies, First Ladies have been there to serve as soothing, calming emotional foundations for their husbands, reminders that they are human beings before they are symbols. Thus we know only from Rose Kennedy's diary that during the days of the Bay of Pigs, the great debacle of her son's Administration, that it was Jackie Kennedy who focused on calming him down and stopping him from endlessly berating himself. From some on the President's staff, there are eyewitness accounts of how, during the tense thirteen days in October 1962 of the Cuban Missile Crisis, Mrs. Kennedy refused to head to a government shelter but to instead stay with her husband in the house, day and night. When it ended, President Kennedy gave her a silver calendar of that month, the days of the crisis deeply engraved. Only his secretary and a handful of advisors and military commanders were shown the same appreciation for helping him through it all. President George W. Bush's strong relationship with his wife helped sustain him through the September 11, 2001 attack on the United States.

Richard Nixon, in the weeks and days preceding his 1974 resignation as president, found it too painful to discuss the effect of the overwhelming Watergate scandal that engulfed him and would not reach out to his wife

Jackie Kennedy whispering to Jack Kennedy at his Inaugural (opposite), **Jackie Kennedy and Nikita Khrushchev** (top left), **Silver calendar given to Jackie "JBK" from JFK marking 13 days of October 1962 missile crisis** (top right), **Jackie Kennedy talking to Russian delegates at post-JFK funeral reception in Red Room** (bottom) Usually defined by her style, Jackie Kennedy was also a woman of political substance. She shared her views on issues, imagery, speeches, personnel with the President, seen here listening to her on Inauguration Day. In May 1961, she met Soviet President Nikita Khrushchev and other members of the Politburo, suggesting to her husband that none of them except Gromyko seemed trustworthy. During the Cuban Missile Crisis, she refused to leave JFK, and he shared with her the intricate details of the nuclear arms standoff with the Soviets. Her supportive role being as important to him as that of his military advisors, he gave her and them the same silver calendar marking the days of the crisis in thanks. She soon after took notes during, and participated in, a private meeting with the President and British Ambassador on nuclear disarmament strategies. At the reception following JFK's funeral, she spoke with the Soviet delegation about how important reducing the arms race had been to him. Before she left the White House, she sent a handwritten note to Khrushchev, reminding him that because of "fear and pride," nuclear war might be started by "little men" who needed the restraint of the Americans and Soviets to prevent it.

A. Frances Cleveland on campaign poster

C. Ida McKinley
campaign button

D. An anti-Eleanor Roosevelt campaign b

E. Mamie Eisenhower
campaign button

B. "Richland County Wants to Make Mrs. Warren G.
Harding First Lady of the Land" paper parachute

F. Jackie Kennedy campaign button

G. Lady Bird Johnson campaign whistle

H. Pat Nixon campaign button

I. Betty Ford campaign button

J. Rosalynn Carter campaign button

K. Nancy Reagan campaign button

L. Barbara Bush campaign button

M. Hillary Clinton
campaign buttons

N. Laura Bush campaign button

A - N Buttons and paraphernalia used the images or names of campaign wives as far back as the 1856 Fremont campaign, but their use become de rigeur after the 1950s.

Eleanor Roosevelt speaking to 1940 Democratic Convention (opposite), **Betty Ford speaking to 1976 Republican Convention** (top), **Republican First Lady Nellie Taft standing between two friends and in front of police at the 1912 Democratic Convention** (bottom) Democrat Eleanor Roosevelt became the first First Lady to address a convention that was nominating her husband for a second term. Pat Nixon was the first to do so at a Republican convention, in 1972. Here, Betty Ford speaks at the following one, in 1976. Edith Wilson was the first Democratic former First Lady to do so (1928), and Nancy Reagan the first Republican one to do so (1996). Laura Bush was the first to do so before she became First Lady, in 2000. Republican Nellie Taft remains the only First Lady to attend the opposition party's convention - and see the man nominated who defeated her husband for re-election.

Pat. In his farewell speech in the East Room, he found that he could not even trust his emotions to mention her, fearing he would break down with the cameras of the world focused on him. In contrast, Andrew Johnson and Bill Clinton both drew upon the stalwart strength of their wives throughout their impeachment trials. In the case of the former, Eliza Johnson, as she told a staff member, "knew he'd be acquitted." In the worst depths of the Great Depression, as everyone seemed to be blaming him personally for the national economic crisis, Herbert Hoover was sustained by Lou Hoover's creation of a nearby mountain retreat (this being prior to the creation of Camp David) and her insistence that he escape for exercise and relief from the stress of the West Wing. As Harry Truman wrote to his wife, "you...must give me help and assistance: because no one ever needed help and assistance as I do now. If I can get...a little help from those I have on a pedestal at home, the job will be done." [15]

In some instances, regardless of how much they served as emotional rocks, some First Ladies were not always successful in breaking the debilitating mood, anger and frustration that beset their Presidents. After the sudden death of their 16-year old son, Calvin Coolidge went into a deep depression that even his bright wife could not break "I hoped to teach him to enjoy life," Grace Coolidge once confessed in discussing his general personality, "He was not very easy to instruct in that way." In other cases, the illnesses or death of their wives so distracted some Presidents that they were unable to carry the full load of their obligations. Jane Pierce's severe depression was so unrelenting that it pervaded her husband's moods and thinking, casting a pall on his Administration. When his beloved first wife Ellen died just as war broke out in Europe, Woodrow Wilson was heard to say, "Oh my God, what am I going to do?" [16]

If emotional influence and support, sound advice and counsel can all have a potential political impact, so too can the highly symbolic role played by First Ladies during presidential campaigns. Not only have most candidates' wives since the latter 19th century been transformed into public figures – willing or not – but many of them have also provided practical advice on everything from speeches to scheduling. A large number of candidates' wives themselves came from families prominent in business or public life of some sort. Simply put, many Presidents "married up." Not only did this make many future First Ladies comfortable in the unusual position of being a private wife placed in the public eye, but also they often had financial, political or other connections of their own. The majority of women who became First Lady were also women ambitious for their husbands to become President: Abigail Adams, Dolley Madison, Louisa Adams, Sarah Polk, Mary Lincoln, Julia Grant, Lucy Hayes, Ida McKinley, Nellie Taft, Ellen Wilson, Florence Harding, Grace Coolidge, Lou Hoover, Mamie Eisenhower, Jacqueline Kennedy, Lady Bird Johnson, Pat Nixon, Rosalynn Carter, Nancy Reagan, Barbara Bush and Hillary Clinton among them.

In the nineteenth century, "campaigning" for one's husband largely took the form of creating a convivial social salon in Washington where the support of individual members of Congress (who served as the nominees of presidential candidates through the election of 1824) was curried. Thus Louisa Adams wrote her husband, she was often in the visitor's gallery of Congress, paying calls on Congressional wives or in some way always, "Smilin' for the presidency." [17] Legendary hostess Dolley Madison was a potent factor in her husband's popularity with the electors. Said Charles Pinckney, who was defeated for the presidency by Madison in 1808, he was "beaten by Mr. and Mrs. Madison. I might have had a better chance had I faced Mr. Madison alone." [18]

Beginning with Mary Lincoln's presence at her husband's campaign rallies and a swing through Ohio, candidates' wives started to appear with their husbands in public, whether on the back of a whistlestop train or the front porch of their own homes. Even before women were given the right to vote, their images began

appearing on buttons and other campaign paraphernalia as an appeal to men who wanted a "family man" or to women who might influence their husbands' votes. With the 1920 campaign, the first national election in which all American women were given the right to vote, Florence Harding began to speak to crowds and her correspondence was crafted to also appeal on "women's issues" such as home economics and the prevention of any international entanglements that might again obligate women to send their men-folk to fight in a foreign war. By the 1950s, an era of mass consumerism, Republican candidates wives Mamie Eisenhower and Pat Nixon were directly "sold" as symbolic images of the post-war boom era to women voters simply by their reflection of the "typical" or "average" housewife. By 1960, Jackie Kennedy even wrote a column "Campaign Wife" touching on politics and tidbits of her private life as a young wife and mother. By 1964, Lady Bird Johnson undertook her own whistlestop tour through the South,

gently raising the issue of racial integration in support of LBJ's Civil Rights Act.

The roles wives have played behind the scenes have been equally helpful to their candidate-husbands. Frequently this has been in the realm of hiring or firing of campaign staff, reviewing the timing and audiences of a candidate's scheduled appearances, gauging the reaction of the media and crowds, and even choosing the photographs or other images to be publicly released of the candidates. Most especially have candidates' wives taken a hand in their husband's speeches. Nellie Taft continually urged her husband not to mention the controversial and confusing tariff in his speeches during the 1908 primary campaign. Jacqueline Kennedy provided numerous historical and literary quotes for her husband's speeches, while Bess Truman censored salty language and impolite references in his. Privately, Mamie Eisenhower strongly voiced her disapproval of speeches her husband made when she felt they were not accessible enough to the average American. "Ike," she interrupted him as he rehearsed one speech, "you can't say that. It's not in character." He angrily continued and she again stopped him. "Ike, that simply isn't you." Twenty minutes followed in which he kept trying to get through the speech and she kept making suggestions. Exasperated, the candidate threw down the speech and never delivered it, according to aide Kevin McCann. [19]

As an extension of this particular campaign role, many women continued to serve as critics or editors of their husbands' speeches once they became President. Rosalynn Carter and Nancy Reagan, for example, advised their husbands not to raise controversial or unpopular subjects in their State of the Union addresses. As revealed on audiotapes of their conversations, Lady Bird Johnson critiqued her husband's speeches with the keenness of a professional journalist, and also urged him to curtail their long-windedness. President Harding once let it slip in public that his wife had helped draft a speech he had just delivered, and she was known to have removed proposals such as American entry in the World Court and a single, six-year presidential term from his State of the Union speeches. Edith Roosevelt long recalled that one of her great regrets was not catching her husband on his election night in 1904 before he announced impromptu to the press that he would refuse to run for another term in 1908; she knew that this could damage his strength as president.

A First Lady can do all this and more without being held accountable, since she is not elected nor held to any specific constitutional duties. The few federal laws governing the activities of a presidential spouse forbid the acceptance of gifts from foreign nations and prohibit the acceptance of domestic gifts or any "financial liabilities" valued over a set price (which increases over time); if such domestic gifts are desired by the spouse they must pay the federal government a market value for them.

No matter how powerful a First Lady may be in her marriage, however, all decisions remain the ultimate responsibility of the President of the United States. In light of the tens of thousands of decisions a President must make, isolated or dramatic examples of their wives' influence, advice, support or

Abraham and Mary Lincoln on Front Porch campaign (opposite top), **Warren and Florence Harding on Front Porch campaign** (opposite bottom), **Harry and Bess Truman on whistlestop tour** (top), **Ellen and Woodrow Wilson on whistlestop tour** (bottom) Campaigning on the front porch of the candidates' home and at whistlestops from the caboose of trains permitted many First Ladies to provide immediate critiques of their husband's speeches and the crowd reaction to what he said. At her Springfield home during a rally, Mary Lincoln can be glimpsed in a window on the front lower left and Florence Harding used her front porch as a personal space to greet women voters. Bess Truman waved to voters with their husband at whistlestops, while Ellen Wilson informally greeted crowds from a train car doorway with her husband.

Pat Nixon during the 1972 convention – with supporters and protestors (top), Jackie Kennedy speaking to women's group during 1960 campaign (bottom), Nancy Reagan surprising husband during debate rehearsal– his re-election television (opposite top), Barbara Bush on campaign plane during 1980 primaries (opposite bottom) As candidates' wives, First Ladies have played a variety of campaign roles. Barbara Bush, popular with reporters, adamantly defended her husband's views during the 1980 Republican primaries. Targeting women voters with whom she was popular, Jackie Kennedy cast issues like elderly medical care and education as necessities that any good daughter or young mother wanted for her parents or children. On the campaign trail, Pat Nixon faced both political supporters and anti-war protestors at the same rally. Nancy Reagan took an especial interest in her husband's preparations for the second of his 1984 televised debates, feeling he had not done well in the first.

counsel does not mean they somehow naturally transform into some version of Lady Mac Beth. It simply means that in varying degrees, a presidential spouse does affect the political process and, in turn, presidential history.

Even First Ladies, however, have found their urgings, influences, and edicts frustrated and slowed by the routine process of the bureaucracy of democracy's checks and balances. "I have waited," Dolley Madison wrote impatiently, "for a speedy appointment from the secretary in favor of W. Williams, but...none...have been made...when is the question that cannot be answered. I will continue to remind him [Cabinet member] of the...merit of the applicant and however tedious the suspense may seem, I think success must crown him at last." [20]

Hillary Clinton meeting with women Senators in 1993 In her first weeks as First Lady, Hillary Clinton held a meeting with the women United States Senators of both parties. Eight years later she would join their ranks. For the first twenty days of 2001, she was simultaneously "the First Lady" and "the Senator," the only presidential spouse ever elected to hold her own political office.

[1] Lewis L. Gould, *Lady Bird Johnson and the Environment* (Lawrence, Kansas: University Press of Kansas, 1988) see pages 157, 159, 162-165, 174-175, 184-185, 190-191 for detailed information on the White House determination to see the bill passed in Congress and the reaction to the effort

[2] Anthony, volume 2, p. 432]

[3] for information on Sarah Polk's political role and views during the Mexican War, see Nelson, pp. 103, 116-117, 143, 199, 259 and 276

[4] quoted in Marianne Means, *The Woman in the White House*, pp. 191, 201-205

[5] Charles Francis Adams, ed., *Works of John Adams* (Boston: Little Brown, 1856) volume 1, p. 547

[6] Marianne Means, pp.248-249

[7] Julia Grant, *Memoirs*, pp. 187, 199

[8] McFeely, Grant, p. 409

[9] Anthony, volume 1, p. 106

[10] Anthony, volume 1, p. 121

[11] Anthony, volume 1, p. 146-147

[12] Means, p. 241

[13] Anthony, volume 2, p. 352; for examples of Ronald Reagan's reliance on his wife's support, see his memoirs, Ronald Reagan, *An American Life* (New York: Simon and Schuster, 1990, pp., 123-124, 167, 184, 380, 389, 536

[14] Anthony, volume 2, p. 276

[15] Coolidge and Truman quotes from Carl Sferrazza Anthony, *America's First Families: An Inside View of 200 Years of Private Life in the White House.* (New York, Touchstone/Simon and Schuster, 2000), p. 82

[16] Anthony, volume 1, p. 349

[17] for information on Louisa Adams' rather extensive campaign advisory role, see Jack Shepard, *Cannibals of the Heart* (New York: McGraw-Hill, 1980) pp. 206-214, 226, 239

[18] Anthony, volume 1, p. 81

[19] "The First Ladies: They've Come a Long Way, Martha, *Smithsonian Magazine*, October 1992

[20] Anthony, volume 1, p. 87

"...I, AND YET NOT I...."

First Ladies, Social Influence and the Popular Culture by Carl Sferrazza Anthony, Author and Historian

> There was a sense of detachment. This was I, and yet not I –
>
> this was the wife of the President and she took precedence over me;
>
> my personal likes and dislikes must be subordinated to the
>
> consideration of those things which were required of her...
>
> -Grace Coolidge

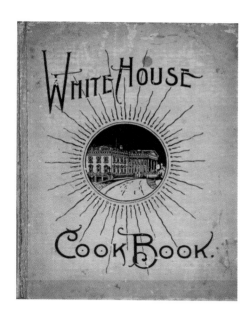

The White House Cookbook (above), **Nancy Reagan tasting food in White House kitchen** (below) The food served to guests at the White House, as well as that favored by the First Families has long seemed to fascinate the public. The first of a number of cookbooks printing the recipes of the First Ladies appeared in the late 1880s. The menus chosen by First Ladies also tend to reflect changing food trends. Nancy Reagan, for example, introduced what was known in the 1980's as the lighter "nouvelle American" cuisine.

In no aspect of life have Americans come to know the First Ladies and their individual qualities more than through their social influences and the popular culture created about them. Thus, the most routine components of any one else's life take on significant, even political implications when applied to the First Ladies. For most of the 19th and early 20th centuries, the First Lady was viewed largely as the hostess and keeper of the White House and the president's life there. What she wore, served her guests, did to the rooms, the technology she used to make life more efficient, what she believed, what sort of music she listened or danced to, what she consumed, read, watched in the theater, how she conducted herself in times of crisis and tragedy – all of it made her an unwitting exemplar for the nation, a role model, and also vulnerable to criticism that was usually politically-motivated.

All of this was apart from how they conducted their private lives – their personal friends, where and how much they spent their money, whether they drank alcohol or smoked tobacco, etc. On occasion, when the public learned of some aspect of their private life or habits (like Jackie Kennedy fox-hunting, or Bess Truman drinking old-fashions, or Dolley Madison pinching tobacco snuff or Julia Grant befriending robber barons or Lucy Hayes singing hymns on Sunday) there would be public reaction, positively or negatively, but it was what they did while "on duty" that attracted the closest notice and seemed to warrant the public's right to commentary.

The notion that perception is as powerful as reality in Washington has particularly seemed to apply to First Ladies. Whether observers among the

public or media read it as some sort of mythical symbolism or as an outright political statement, the manner in which a First Lady not only shapes her personal image but also that of the President and the White House can impact the impression formed of an Administration. It is hard to imagine the idea of "Camelot" or the Kennedy Administration as being that of John F. Kennedy alone: Jackie Kennedy gave it subtle and profound definition – in the food and entertainment she gave her guests, in the way she dressed herself as well as in the way she saw to it that the President dressed appropriately and often what his remarks were. The frenzied and shocking early days of the New Deal was perpetuated as much by Eleanor Roosevelt's

kinetic and nervous sense of purpose as it by was the "alphabet soup" agencies immediately established by presidential initiative. The tragedy of the Lincoln years, the elegance of the Reagan period, the Calvinistic zeal in the White House during the Mexican War, the mannered Europeanism of Monroe's Era of Good Feeling, the loose front-porch neighborliness of the Harding term – so many presidencies were moulded by that intangible idea of "style," and most of that sense of style came from First Ladies.

The most immediately visible badge of a First Lady's self-created image is, as it seems always to have been – her clothes. From the earliest days of

Betty Ford doing the "Hustle" dance in 1970s Popular dances throughout the decades have sometimes been tried out by the First Ladies themselves: Julia Tyler introduced the polka to Washington society; Mary Lincoln danced the quadrille; Grace Coolidge tried the Charleston in private with her sons; Jackie Kennedy did the Twist. Here, Betty Ford tries the 1970s move of "the Hustle" with singer Tony Orlando.

Julia Grant receiving guests (top), **Grant family china** (bottom)
Julia Grant entertained lavishly in the Gilded Age, often welcoming many of the industrial robber barons of the era. She maintained several different sets of china, an official one for the White House and a private one she used for her family, pieces of which are seen here.

the presidency, what the First Ladies wore and how well they looked in them were a matter of consuming interest.

Martha Washington let out the word – or someone around her did – that she wore dresses made from the rewoven silk of old chair-covers and other recycled cloth. True or not, it reinforced her image as a practical woman who never wasted nor wanted. Dolley Madison's taking to the popular French style of low-cut gowns in flimsy cloth raised many an eyebrow, particularly since her figure filled it out so generously. Julia Tyler's clothes were minutely described in newspaper articles, as were those of her immediate successor Sarah Polk, both of whom dressed in sumptuous outfits, clearly seeing themselves as queen-like figures. The long-sleeved high-neck dresses of Lucy Hayes served as a conscious reinforcement of the pious tone by which she and her husband sought to define his Administration. The fact that Edith Wilson dressed in gowns by the Paris house of Worth was a fact well publicized during her accompaniment to France for the Versailles Treaty. Grace Coolidge consciously dressed in modulated versions of the "flapper" style dresses of the 1920s, making her seem contemporary yet comparatively conservative. Mamie Eisenhower perfectly mirrored the high style of the 1950s with her bright colors and girlish costumes – including faux jewelry, and the styles of her hats were so well known that she was the only First Lady ever voted to the best "hatted" list.

First Ladies are conscious of the fact that the public and the press scrutinized their appearances and were role models of fashion whether they enjoyed such a privilege or not (and many have not). It was not long into the institution of the presidency that this occurred. "At my age I think I am privileged to set a fashion," Abigail Adams wrote, "So far as example goes, I shall bring in the use of silks." [1]

Numerous trends have been credited to several First Ladies: Dolley Madison and the turban; Harriet Lane and the "bertha," a lace covering over the bodices of plunging gowns; Frances Cleveland and the demise of the bustle. In the twentieth century such styles were easier to document through the "women's pages" of newspapers. Despite the fact that she was an older woman, Florence Kling Harding's signature use of a black satin neckpiece (to cover her wrinkles) was copied by debutantes briefly in the early twenties as "Flossie clings" because, as one reporter put it, they were "flossy and they cling." During the Depression, Lou Hoover attempted to aid the failing cotton industry by dressing in all-cotton evening gowns. Mamie Eisenhower's frequent use of the color "Mamie Pink" reinforced the idea of it as a popular feminine color of the 1950s. Barbara Bush's public appearances in three-strand pearls, both fake and real, prompted numerous companies to copy them, at least one of which used a look-alike of Mrs. Bush posing for a "First Lady pearls" ad.

No First Lady had a greater impact on fashion than Jackie Kennedy. Her gowns, hats, gloves, purses, sportswear, sunglasses – all were copied not only by thousands of individual women but also by manufacturers who specifically copied and marketed her style. She herself had a sense of this. "I know that I am so much more of fashion interest than other First Ladies," she wrote her designer Oleg Cassini, "[but I] refuse to have Jack's administration plagued by fashion stories of a sensational nature - & and to be the Marie Antoinnette or Josephine of the 1960s…" [2]

Other First Ladies have found themselves the target of such exploitation. Louisa Adams was eagerly sent a bonnet with the hope that she would wear it and make it popular – and tell admirers the name of the manufacturer. Sarah Polk and Mary Lincoln were also sent headgear with the same intention.

Some First Ladies found themselves the unwitting targets of critical editorials and media coverage based on their clothing, perhaps seeking to make political hay out of it. Mary Lincoln told her dressmaker Elizabeth Keckley that, "I must dress in costly materials. The people scrutinize every article that I wear with critical curiosity." Her extravagance during the Civil War, however, did nothing to reduce the criticisms. When she appeared at one reception in a low-cut gown and her customary headpiece of fresh roses, an Oregon senator maliciously described her as having "her bosom on exhibition and a flowerpot on her head." [3]

The media fixated on Nancy Reagan's designer gowns during the 1981 recession and raised legal questions about her acceptance of clothes as "gifts." The Women's Christian Temperance Union petitioned Frances Cleveland to stop wearing what they considered the immoral low-cut gowns she favored. Finally, the First Ladies' manner of dress also reflected the evolutions of everything from gender roles to textile manufacturing. Lucy Hayes, for example, wore intricate gowns weighed down by steel beading cut by factory machinery; Eleanor Roosevelt used synthetic materials in her hose during the wartime silk shortage. In 1972, Pat Nixon was the first First Lady to pose for fashion pages in pants. By 2003, Laura Bush had so frequently appeared in pants in both formal and informal outfits that it provoked little to no comment.

Hairstyle has even come in for its alleged newsworthiness, whether it was Frances Cleveland's shaved neck nape and loose hair knot covering it, Bess Truman's gray "poodle cut," Mamie Eisenhower's bangs, Jackie Kennedy's bouffant or Barbara Bush's natural snow-white color. After what seemed to be endless stories in the Washington Post about Hillary Clinton's changing hairstyle, the exasperated First Lady

Cartoon of Lucy Hayes in liquor bottle and water bottle In contrast to her immediate successor Julia Grant who openly served the intoxicating "Roman Punch" to guests, temperance adherent "Lemonade Lucy" Hayes served no alcoholic beverages of any kind. She is satirized in a cartoon here – dour in a wine bottle, smiling in a water bottle.

Invitation to the Tafts' Silver Wedding Anniversary Many of the guests invited to the gargantuan lawn party that Nellie Taft held for her 1911 silver wedding anniversary at the White House were politically or financially powerful individuals— and potential supporters and convention delegates for her husband's 1912 re-election campaign.

finally remarked, "All I have to do to get Bosnia off the front page is to change my hairdo."

In a far less specific manner, the interior design and decorating tastes of First Ladies as reflected in the public rooms of the White House have taken on political consequence. Although she was not mentioned by name, Angelica Van Buren's honeymoon trip to the royal courts of Europe, concurrent but not in any way related to the White House redecoration by her father-in-law, the widowed President, became an issue of attack in the famous "Gold Spoon" speech of Pennsylvania Congressmen Charles Ogle. Edith Roosevelt's reclaiming of classical design in the state rooms, following the White House 1902 renovation, sought to establish an imperial tone in synch with an America that was now a world power. Jackie Kennedy's restoration of the White House rooms was heralded as a new era in the budding historic preservation movement, one of the issues by which her husband's Administration became identified. That Lucretia Garfield, Lucy Hayes, Grace Coolidge and Lou Hoover also initiated historic preservation efforts went unmentioned in the media covering the Kennedy effort: there had been little public consciousness about genuine historic preservation in their times. When Hillary Clinton unveiled her redecoration of the Blue Room just weeks after the health care reform effort she headed collapsed, some in the press reported that she had assumed the decorating project as a way of "softening" her public image from politician to hostess (in fact, such efforts involve the approval of committees and take considerable time). Conversely, the run-down quality of the state rooms during the Great Depression and World War II provoked some tourists to criticize Eleanor Roosevelt as being negligent of her basic duties as housekeeper, regardless of the social activism role she had assumed.

The form of entertainment hosted and the guests invited by the President and First Lady has also been viewed through a political spectrum. These include Mary Lincoln's lavish receptions during wartime, Rosalynn Carter's barbeque picnics, Frances Cleveland's Saturday receptions for working-class women, Nellie Taft's inviting of Republican leaders and potential convention delegates to her silver anniversary a year before her husband's run for re-election, Lou Hoover's welcoming of the first African-American congressional wife invited to a tea, Hillary Clinton's St. Patrick's Day events at which both representatives of both Ireland and Northern Ireland were guests.

Even the food and drink that First Ladies served to guests became the subject of public commentary. Eleanor Roosevelt received critical reactions after she served what she considered quintessentially American food – frankfurters – to the King and Queen of England. When Nancy Reagan's office accidentally sent her recipe for an expensive appetizer to a woman writing for advice on how to feed her family on a limited income, it became an item of interest to the media. In at least one situation, a First Lady decided to respond directly. After the snobbish wife of the British Ambassador commented that the buffet tables of simple, country foods that Dolley Madison, acting as Jefferson's official hostess, served was like a "harvest home supper," she shot back, "The profusion of my table arises from the happy circumstance of abundance and prosperity in our country." [4]

While Sarah Polk and Rosalynn Carter decided against serving hard liquor and Lucy Hayes didn't serve any alcohol, those who did serve it sometimes came in for attack. Nellie Taft ignored letters begging her to stop serving her champagne punch and her steadfastness earned her at least one supportive editorial. Lucretia Garfield strongly resisted the pleas of angry temperance advocates who had expected her to continue the Hayes custom. In contrast, Jackie Kennedy's inauguration of open cocktail bars at receptions earned her the support of powerful syndicated society columnist Betty Beale. How former and incumbent First Ladies coped with the 18th Amendment of Prohibition also reflects on the varying attitudes toward the controversial law. Most of those who were former First Ladies during Prohibition– Frances Cleveland, Edith Roosevelt, Nellie Taft, and Edith Wilson – refused to comply on principal. Incumbents Grace Coolidge, Lou Hoover and Eleanor Roosevelt complied, while Florence Harding seemed to strike a compromise, serving and mxing alcoholic drinks in the private quarters but never to the public in the state rooms or on the lawn.

Beyond the consideration of how such "style" was translated into political substance, an overview of White House life as dictated by First Ladies is a weathervane of popular trends and movements widespread through the nation. In terms of technology one sees examples of this in Sarah Polk's resistance to gas lighting and Caroline Harrison's mistrust of electrical lighting, Nellie Taft's insistence on automobiles transporting her and her family instead of the old horse-and carriages, Frances Cleveland using her own "brownie" portable camera, Florence Harding owning a radio and riding in an airplane, Mamie Eisenhower clearing her schedule to watch favorite television shows, even Rosalynn Carter bringing in the first VCR to the family quarters. This weathervane is equally apparent in what First Ladies personally enjoyed – whether it was Florence

Louisa Adams on the arm of General Jackson at reception (opposite top), **Eleanor Roosevelt serving tea and cake** (opposite bottom), **Jackie Kennedy with Robert Frost at state dinner entertainment** (below) Numerous First Ladies used their hostess role for purposes beyond entertaining. Louisa Adams, on the arm of General Jackson, specifically focused on cultivating Congressmen as potential supporters for her husband's 1824 presidential race – the last election that had Congress serving as the electors. Eleanor Roosevelt initially dreaded the social role – until she realized how powerful a political perk a White House invitation could be, and how important a symbol she was in the position of hostess. Jackie Kennedy reveled in her hostess role and used the post-dinner entertainment to showcase American performance arts, underlining her effort to forge a government agency that supported the arts.

Harding indulging in the Twenties obsession for mahjong and Eskimo pies, Nancy Reagan trying "the new Coca-Cola" and even break-dancing, Betty Ford getting a mood ring and doing "the hustle" dance move, Hillary Clinton having the mansion decorated at Christmas by popular entertaining guru Martha Stewart, or Jackie Kennedy dancing the Twist at private parties and playing bossa-nova albums on her "hi-fi." Julia Tyler became so closely associated with the new dance of the "polka" that a series of dances were even named for her. Even Jane Pierce's and Mary Lincoln's use of famous mediums to contact their dead relatives corresponds to a mid-Victorian age craze with spiritualism.

Beginning with the Wilson era, First Ladies seemed to have as great a fascination with "movie stars" and Hollywood feature films as did the rest of the nation. Edith Wilson was placed on equal status with the likes of actress Mabel Norman during a World War I fundraiser in Washington. Florence Harding was the first to use a feature film, "Covered Wagon," as entertainment following a state dinner. Grace Coolidge went out to the public theaters to catch the latest "moving picture shows," an apparent fan of heartthrob Rudolph Valentino like thousands of other American women at the time. Eleanor Roosevelt regularly screened Hollywood films for her family and personal guests in the White House, including the popular 1939 picture, "Gone With the Wind." During the Roosevelt, Truman, Kennedy, Johnson,

Photo courtesy of the Collection Of The New-York Historical Society

Dolley Madison portrait with turban (top left), **Harriet Lane wearing the low-neck lace bertha** (top right), **Frances Cleveland in low-cut dress with no bustle** (bottom left), **Grace Coolidge smiling at ballgame in white sports wear** (opposite top left), **Lou Hoover posing in cotton dress** (opposite top right), **Jackie Kennedy fixing her hair in a mirror** (opposite bottom) For much of the history of the presidency, First Ladies were observed for their clothing style and sometimes became role models, setting trends. Dolley Madison's signature turban was copied by many Washington women as would be Harriet Lane's "bertha," a suggestive lace covering for her plunging neckline. Frances Cleveland's lowcut gowns brought the wrath of the WCTU, which petitioned her to stop being a bad example for young girls; later, when reporters falsely claimed that she had stopped wearing the bustle, that style so quickly became passé that even she stopped wearing it. Grace Coolidge, a baseball fan, hiker and swimmer, often appeared in the new lines of lighter sportswear for women. During the Depression, Lou Hoover wore cotton dresses with the intention of trying to set a trend for them and help spur the cotton industry. Jackie Kennedy's famous bouffant hairstyle was copied by millions of women.

Nixon and Ford years, the most popular actors of the moment were frequently invited as guests to the White House. In the 1980's, with both the First Lady and President having been Hollywood actors, a wide spectrum of stars were at the White House, from legends such as Jimmy Stewart, Bob Hope and Ginger Rogers to more contemporary figures like Tom Cruise, Cher and Michael Jackson. During the Clinton years, many actors were invited for a screening of their latest films in the White House movie theater.

A sense that the White House is either practically or symbolically in touch with what the "average" American household is going through at any given time is an important political factor; no Administration wants to appear insensitive to, or avoiding what the rest of the nation may be experiencing.

Since the First Lady is still considered the manager of the house, domestic decisions are still credited to her direction. During wartime, for example, Edith Wilson instituted special days when her household sacrificed meat, gasoline or other necessities, as the rest of the American people were required to do. It was this ideal of sacrifice that is at the heart of what Dolley Madison did when the British burned the White House when she rescued national icons but left her personal possessions behind to be destroyed.

Other First Ladies have dealt with the tempo of their times in similar ways. Margaret Taylor kept her slaves in the mansion, out of sight from the public view at a time of growing sectionalism and mounting tension over the spread of slavery in new states and territories. Florence Harding led a boycott on sugar when prices became too exorbitant for most American households. Bess Truman signed "the housewife's pledge" to limit usage of food staples at a time of global postwar shortages. Eleanor Roosevelt kept the entire White House on the strict wartime rationing system that the government instituted during World War II. During the Vietnam War, Lady Bird Johnson saw off her two son-in-laws, one of whom was placed at the front, just as thousands of other families sent off the men in their families. Laura Bush managed to balance White House social life in the post-"9-11" period of terrorism: no excessive entertaining or celebrating yet keeping to previously scheduled events, including the traditional White House holiday sea-

Nellie Taft with the President in her automobile (top right), **Florence Harding at right in flying outfit before ascending in a hydro plane**(above), **Herbert and Lou Hoover listening to the radio** (middle left), **Grace Coolidge with home movie camera** (opposite) Technological innovations have often been eagerly embraced by First Ladies and, in the process, became unintentional symbols promoting the product or industry: Nellie Taft insisted on having a fleet of automobiles for the use of her presidential family instead of the old horse-and-carriages. Florence Harding was the first First Lady to fly in an airplane. Grace Coolidge enjoyed taking her own home movies with a newfangled portable "moving picture" camera. Although the Hardings were the first in the White House to have a radio, Lou Hoover was so enamored with the invention that she began making frequent speeches through the new technology.

Drawing of Elizabeth Keckley sewing Mary Lincoln's dress (opposite top left), **Elizabeth Keckley book cover** (opposite top right), **Eleanor Roosevelt at Howard University with two African-American escorts** (opposite bottom left), **Cover of book, "Weep No More My Lady..."** (opposite bottom right), **Lady Bird Johnson on the back train platform of the "Lady Bird Special" in South** (below) Most of the First Ladies came from wealthy backgrounds whose only early exposure to African-Americans was in their capacity as slaves or servants. Nevertheless, many of them felt strongly about helping to forge civil rights. Witness to the slave trade in her native Kentucky, Mary Lincoln closely befriended her White House seamstress Elizabeth Keckley and through her came to support the Contraband Relief Society, which provided shelter, food, education and employment for runaway slaves. She also became an outspoken abolitionist. When Keckley later published her memoirs, however, Mrs. Lincoln felt betrayed. Eleanor Roosevelt became a friend of many black leaders, successfully pushed for more employment integration in the federal government, joined protests against segregation and spoke out vigorously on the need for equal rights for African-Americans. When the picture of her being escorted by two African-American men during her visit to Howard University appeared, there was a backlash of attacks, particularly from the South. The anti-Eleanor Roosevelt book *Weep No More My Lady* was published by segregationalists in response to one of her columns. During her husband's 1964 presidential campaign, Lady Bird Johnson made a whistlestop tour of her own throughout the southern states, speaking as a southerner, but making the convincing case that the Civil Rights Acts would move all people – black and white – ahead.

son, as a means of illustrating practical caution with "living a normal life."

Similarly, during the fears of flying provoked by the Gulf War, Barbara Bush made a symbolic flight on a commercial airline rather than travel as usual on the secure Air Force planes at her disposal. Even if the action is clearly only symbolic – Barbara Bush, for example, resumed flying on the secure planes after her initial commercial flight – it is appreciated by the public and recognized for what it is, a sign of solidarity with the general public. Mrs. Bush was exemplar at the single symbolic act. During the height of the AIDS crisis, she placed candles in all the windows of the White House, as others were doing in Washington, to show her and the President's sensitivity to the personal losses. When she learned that the bell-ringing Salvation Army volunteers at a nearby shopping mall were about to be evicted at the holiday time as a nuisance, she made a trip to the mall, just to drop some money in their canister and register her support. Ultimately, the bell-ringers were not removed. Rosalynn Carter, frustrated by her inability to change the mood caused by the Iranian Hostage Crisis, decided to tie a yellow ribbon (a spontaneous sign of remembrance of loved ones who are gone) on a small tree on the North Lawn of the White House which tourists emerging from the mansion would pass. When a First Lady seems too self-absorbed or removed from the realities of life at the time, a simple act or reaction can have detrimental consequences. When Mary Lincoln went into deep mourning upon the death of her 11-year old son Willie, there was a negative reaction in a nation that was losing its sons daily in a civil war being managed by her husband.

The actions of several other First Ladies were intentional yet subtle enough to avoid outright controversy. During the Depression, Lou Hoover spent much of her own considerable wealth in helping the poor and unemployed with financial support of basic needs and even created and funded a small rural schoolhouse. In this way, she made herself a living example of the voluntary methods President Hoover was promoting as a means of coping with the economic crisis, as opposed to government welfare programs. In the midst of some of the most heated and violent resistance to racial integration in public education, Jackie Kennedy established a White House kindergarten for her daughter with carefully chosen schoolmates that included the African-American son of the President's assistant press secretary. Without making an actual verbal statement, the First Lady permitted photographs of the schoolchildren together to be publicly released, putting her in perfect accord with the Administration's Justice Department's rulings on integration. Even when there was just a period of time when an Administration was initiating new policy, First Ladies have coordinated their efforts to visually illustrate the point being made by their husband's initiative. During a trip to the Midwest, for example, when President Nixon was propounding his environmental reclamation policy, Pat Nixon left Washington with him, but then went off on her own to inspect reclaimed strip mining fields.

In this way, First Ladies' "special projects" have also served the political purposes of the Administration while bringing attention to a social ill

Edith Wilson, second from right, serving coffee to WWI soldiers off to war at train station (opposite top left), **President Bush and Laura Bush comfort family members at Washington Hospital Center Sept. 13, 2001**(opposite top right), **Lady Bird Johnson looking over urban renewal model of Washington, DC** (opposite bottom), **Betty Ford and Vietnamese refugee children and orphans** (top), **Rosalynn Carter tying a yellow ribbon around tree for Iranian hostages** (middle left), **Barbara Bush looking at AIDS quilt** (middle right) Throughout times of crisis, wartime or social problems, a First Lady can be a symbol of leadership and also make political points by sharing the burden, grief and sacrifice with the public at large. During World War I, Edith Wilson – seen on previous page in a Red Cross uniform serving coffee to outgoing soldiers – instituted days at the White House when meats weren't served for dinner or car drives weren't taken to save gasoline, as the rest of the nation did. Although it came under the umbrella of her "beautification" efforts, Lady Bird Johnson studied and weighed in on 1960s urban renewal efforts in the capital city. In the days that followed the airlifts out of Vietnam, Betty Ford was on hand to meet and comfort some of the thousands of orphans and young children brought to the United States without their parents; like many Americans, she also considered possibly adopting one of the children. During the Iranian Hostage Crisis, Rosalynn Carter, like tens of thousands of other citizens, tied a yellow ribbon of remembrance around a tree on the White House lawn. Barbara Bush met with a family who lost a member to AIDS and brought into the White House a piece of the massive AIDS quilt displayed on the Washington Mall, made to remember the thousands of Americans who died of the illness. Laura Bush, in the Capitol Building that was likely an intended target of terrorists on "9-11" when other sites were hit, visited Washington Hospital Center with the President on September 13, 2001. The President and First Lady visited the hospital to thank doctors and visit patients wounded in the attack on the Pentagon.

prevalent at the time. Although Nancy Reagan began her anti-drug use awareness campaign among young school students without involving herself in policy, by the end of the Administration (and the pervasive use of drugs by even "respectable" segments of society like Wall Street stockbrokers on lunch breaks), she was addressing the entire United Nations general assembly on drug trafficking, global interdiction and other elements of the Reagan Administration policy as a State Department messenger. Although Lady Bird Johnson had long been interested in gardening, outdoor life and natural beauty, it was only after hearing her husband deliver a June 1964 speech on environmental policy at the University of Michigan that she decided to coordinate her

own "special project" with the Administration's efforts. It also reflected a growing national concern for the environment, culminating in the last year of the Johnson Administration with the creation of "Earth Day." As she recalled, "We have misused our resources, but we haven't destroyed them. It is late. It is fortunately not too late…" [5]

In other, more personal ways that are entirely unplanned, First Ladies can also find themselves suddenly being heralded as role models of behavior. In the case of two women who were widowed through assassination, this role took on dramatic proportions. Throughout the ten weeks between the July morning President Garfield was shot and wounded until his death at the cooling shore in September, Lucretia Garfield's strength, confidence and support of her husband earned her universal admiration from the nation. Readers learned the details of those anxious summer dog days in the swampy capital through the daily bulletins of newspaper correspondents posted at the mansion. She was held up as a "representative American woman" in some editorials. "She fitly represents the best qualities of her sex, and is an honor to a nation, which, more highly than any other in the world, esteems women,' concluded one newspaper clipping preserved in her personal papers. [6] In the end, in a spontaneous act of national sympathy for Mrs. Garfield and the five children she had to support and put through school, citizens raised a $360,000 fund for her.

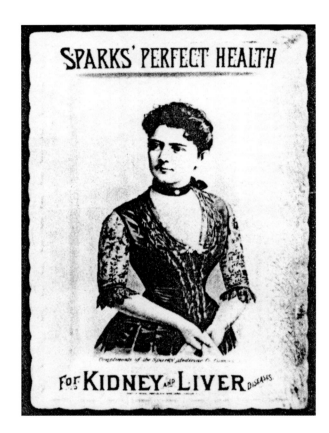

In the four days of November 1963, from the moment the news broke that President Kennedy had been killed until his burial at Arlington National Cemetery, the widowed First Lady seized the attention of the entire world. The public face she put on of bravery and strength, along with her dramatic gestures such as walking behind the caisson carrying her husband's flag-draped coffin to the lighting of an eternal flame at his gravesite turned her into a national heroine and a figure of admiration that quickly turned into near deification. Occurring as it did during the relatively new phenomena of television, the assassination and the events which followed it unwittingly thrust Jackie Kennedy into a dubious status of recognition that none of her successors or predecessors ever experienced, that of a "pop icon." Earlier signs of such a status, however, were apparent from the first days of the Administration.

In the consumer culture of the late 1950s and early 1960s, the physical youth and beauty, glamour and perceived life of ease that Jackie Kennedy learned to consciously cultivate as First Lady found its way into all forms of commercial exploitation. Toys, clothing, humorous novelty items, everyday household goods all carried the imprint of Jackie Kennedy. Various lines of First Lady dolls had been made by outfits such as the popular "Madame Alexander," but with Jackie Kennedy came a plethora of others – for girls to play with and for older women to collect and dress. Spoons, plates, mugs, glasses, perfume, wall plaques, bottle-tops, planters, luggage, comedy records, even a rock-and-roll song, "The Jackie Look," were just a few of the sort of items churned out with the visage of the First Lady. Even as late as 2003, in "The Vermont Country Store" catalogue, for example, its "sweet almond oil" is advertised as "Jackie Kennedy's Secret to Silky-Soft Skin, Clear Complexion."

Jackie Kennedy was even the cover story subject of numerous gossip magazines that had previously focused only on movie stars; this seemed to open the floodgates to later generations of tabloids that printed lurid and wild rumors and exaggerated speculations about some of her successors such as Nancy Reagan, Barbara Bush, Hillary Clinton and Laura Bush.

Such openness, along with a permissiveness that followed the alienation and mistrust of government figures after the Vietnam War and Watergate scandals made the First Ladies not only subject to unseemly reporting but worthy of political satire. The more they became involved in political issues or served as political symbols, the more they were skewered.

Since the 1980s, First Ladies had earned the backhanded compliment of becoming instantly recognizable figures. There had been ugly jokes and cartoons, voice parodies and impersonations of Eleanor Roosevelt (notably as the last line in the 1942 film version of *The Man Who Came to Dinner*) [7], Pat Nixon (on the comedy album "I Am the President" by Nixon impersonator David Frye), humorously spliced voice tracks of Lady Bird Johnson (on the Earle Doud record label series) and Marx Toys figurines and cream pitchers shaped from a bust of Mamie Eisenhower. At the end of the twentieth century, however, First Ladies were outrightly caricatured in products. Thus in the 1980s, 1990s and first decade of the 21st century, Americans could buy rubber masks, salt-and-pepper shakers, bedroom slippers, bobbing-head dolls, squeeze dolls, greeting cards,

Advertisement for Lucy Hayes and steam iron (opposite top), **Frances Cleveland ashtray advertising "Kidney and Liver Pills"** (opposite middle), **Caroline Harrison corset fastener advertisement** (below) Without seeking their permission, manufacturers simply used the faces or names of late 19th century First Ladies as celebrity promoters of their goods. Thus Lucy Hayes pushed steam irons, France Cleveland sold kidney and liver pills, and Caroline Harrison hawked girdle fasteners – with no less a person than Queen Victoria.

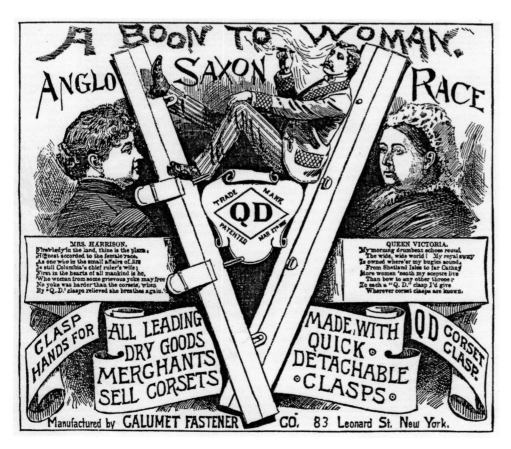

and even hot sauce with cartooned versions of the faces of Nancy Reagan, Barbara Bush, Hillary Clinton and Laura Bush.

What makes this different from earlier commercial use of First Ladies is that the names and faces of Martha Washington, Abigail Adams, Dolley Madison and Mary Lincoln had been appropriated for traditionally feminine products: powders, make-up, dessert foods, flour, sugar, tea and coffee, and china, stemware, flatware, dress, curtain, upholstery and wallpaper patterns. Whether it was "Martha Washington soap," "Dolly Madison wine" or "Mary Lincoln candies," it was intended as tribute to their hostess and housekeeping skills. However romanticized their posthumous images might have been, the intent of appeal to the women of the early- to mid-20th century was clearly that the products represented the finest quality, worthy of memorializing the most legendary ladies of the White House. Even at the end of the century, however, products portraying these women were domestic in nature: dinner bells made in the shapes of Abigail Adams, Dolley Madison and Mary Lincoln, ceramic doll heads based on Florence Harding, Grace Coolidge and Lou Hoover, an enamel pin in the shape of Bess Truman and even a whiskey bottle in the shape of Eleanor Roosevelt. A 2003 on-line catalogue still carries the white cotton "First Lady Bedspread" inspired by one used by Abigail Adams.

Only one previous First Lady had experienced a level of exploitation in the 19th century that was comparable to what Jackie Kennedy experienced in the 20th century. As the 21-year old beautiful brunette bride of the President, Frances Folsom Cleveland became an overnight sensation, a national celebrity for Gilded Age and Gay 90's America, especially young women. Advertisements selling liver and arsenic pills, luggage, sewing machines, tobacco products, soaps and numerous other products bought largely by women freely appropriated the face of the new First Lady. It was considered such an outrageously un-chivalrous act against a lady that a Congressional bill forbidding the unapproved use of any image of any American woman was considered, but it got no where. Frances Cleveland faced the same dilemma Jackie Kennedy would: there was no legal action short of a reprimand that could be taken to stop the exploiters. President Cleveland could not help himself in writing one Leo Oppenheim, who Cleveland said had used his wife's image in "the most indecent way" in an *Albany Evening Journal* advertisement. "I suppose we must always have...dirty and disreputable fellows, but I shall be surprised if you find such advertising profitable..." [8]

When Frances Cleveland left the White House in 1897, there would never be that sort of commercialization she experienced until Mrs. Kennedy. If older and less glamorous First Ladies did not quite spark the fascination that the younger woman did, however, it was not for lack of trying. Nellie Taft found herself a face on a souvenir plate, a short-lived series that produced

Frances Cleveland – Queen of Hearts card (top), **Rosalynn Carter – Queen of Diamonds card** (middle) In the 19th century, Frances Cleveland as the Queen of Hearts in a deck of political playing cards simply reflected her popularity. A century later, Rosalynn Carter as the Queen of Diamonds satirized her political influence.

Mary Lincoln candy box (above), Dolley Madison cigar box (bottom), First Ladies tin cookie box (right) The lines of numerous personal, entertaining household, and food products – powders, makeup, furniture, lamps, draperies, bedspreads, china, crystal, cutlery, cookies, candies, ice cream, coffee, tea, wine – have long appropriated the names of 19th century First Ladies, marketing these legendary hostesses to the consumer hostesses. That a line of cigars would be named for Dolley Madison seems odd – until one recalls her own addiction to tobacco snuff.

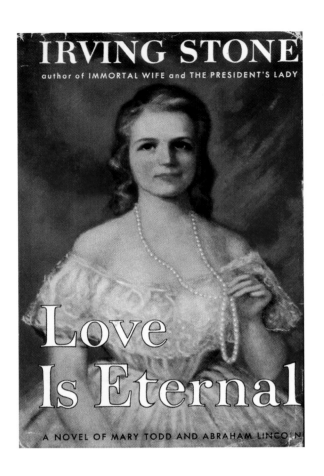

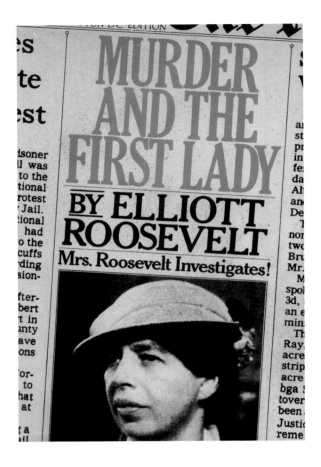

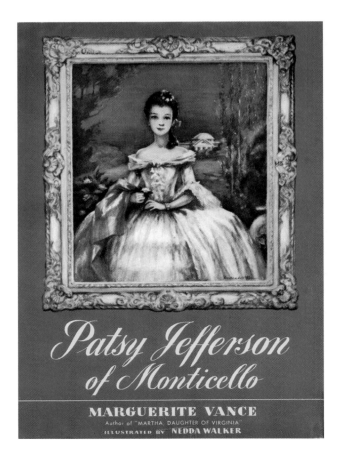

Cover of "Love is Eternal" by Irving Stone (top left), **Cover of "Murder and the First Lady" by Elliott Roosevelt** (top right), **Cover of children's book, "Patsy Jefferson of Monticello"** (bottom left) Fictional accounts of First Ladies written with some factual basis have been published since the 1940s. Irving Stone novels about the romances of Abigail Adams, Mary Lincoln, and Rachel Jackson that were extremely popular and the last of the three titles was made into a movie. Elliott Roosevelt penned a series of "Eleanor Roosevelt Murder Mysteries," about his mother. The lives of not only presidential wives but at least one presidential daughter – Martha Jefferson Randolph – were frequently used as the subject of children's books.

Edith Roosevelt and Ida McKinley as well. For the matronly women of "the Anglo-Saxon race," one advertisement even posed Queen Victoria alongside grandmotherly Caroline Harrison in an ad for girdle fasteners.

Before even Frances Cleveland had become First Lady, there had been a more subtle and thus, perhaps, acceptable form of exploiting the president's wife – as thinly veiled characters in popular fiction. The first, aforementioned, example was Margaret Smith's novel *What Is Gentility?* for which the author sought and gained permission from one of those she based a character on – Dolley Madison. Author and historian Henry Adams – grandson of Lousia Adams and great-grandson of Abigail Adams – wrote what many consider to be the first political novel, *Democracy*. Although his First Lady character is only mentioned in passing, it is based on Julia Grant, with all the fumbling foibles and savvy instincts that the real woman possessed. As he wrote in the novel, "There was much interest among the ladies in reading of the lives of early Presidents' wives. Those who knew realized that the power itself lay in their province."

In the early twentieth century children's and young adult books on First Ladies seemed to say more about popular reading and women's roles during a particular era than they did to accurately translate the lives of First Ladies for junior readers. Martha Washington, Abigail Adams, Dolley Madison and Mary Lincoln are invariably drawn as good housekeepers or girls interested in becoming good wives in colonial or frontier America. Only after the 1962 death of Eleanor Roosevelt and the post-1963 fascination with Jackie Kennedy did children and young adult books seek to make First Ladies appear as role models who balanced the traditional expectations of private life with the unusual expectations of public life. Now there are young adult books on women as diverse as Sarah Polk, Frances Cleveland, Harriet Lane, Nellie Taft, Betty Ford, Hillary Clinton and Laura Bush.

In the mid-twentieth century, author Irving Stone generated a new type of interest in First Ladies with his romance stories of three presidential couples, *The President's Lady* (Rachel and Andrew Jackson), *Love is Eternal* (Mary and Abraham Lincoln) and *Those Who Love* (Abigail and John Adams). The books were such best sellers that they often became the first and only exposure many otherwise occupied Americans had to these historical figures. Within the next half-century, there was a plethora of novels using First Ladies as characters, notably Jacqueline Suzanne's book *Dolores*, about Jackie Kennedy and even the thriller, *How the Greeks Kidnapped Mrs. Nixon*, about a plot by Greek militants who took power in the 1970s and captured the American First Lady for ransom. Elliott Roosevelt made humorous use of his mother's deductive sensibilities in the Eleanor Roosevelt murder mystery series. Feminist novelist Rita Mae Brown celebrated the zesty life of her fellow Virginian in *Dolley*, and there was even a romance novel imagining life from the perspective of the most obscure presidential wife, Martha Jefferson, who died twenty years before her husband became president.

Television and feature film portrayals have been far less successful than novels in conveying the full breath and depth of First Ladies' stories. Part of

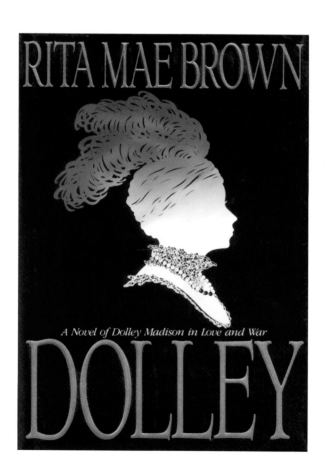

Cartoon color illustration from *Dolley Madison's Surprise* (top left), **Photograph still of movie *"Magnificent Doll"* with Ginger Rogers** (top right), **Cover of *"Dolley a novel of Dolley Madison in Love and War"*** (bottom left) Dolley Madison has always been a favorite subject of the popular imagination, whether it be for a humorous children's book crediting her with introducing ice cream, a movie role in which the blonde Ginger Rodgers played the black-haired First Lady, or a novel.

the dilemma is that the President is usually the main character and thus the characterization of his wife is always a supportive and less-developed role. On television, there were accurate and complex scripts and portrayals in *Eleanor and Franklin*, starring Jane Alexander, a mini-series based on the same-titled book by Joseph P. Lash, and the *Betty Ford Story*, starring Gena Rollins, the storyline of which the former First Lady personally worked in helping to develop. Those few feature films, all made in the 1930s, 1940s or 1950s, that had First Ladies as characters tended to make them overly glamorous (as when slim Susan Hayward played the corpulent Rachel Jackson in *The President's Lady*), overly comic (blonde Ginger Rodgers playing the black-haired Dolley Madison in *The Magnificent Doll*), overly dramatic (Ruth Gordon as a querulous Mary Lincoln in *Lincoln of Illinois*), or overly noble (Geraldine Fitzgerald as Edith Wilson in *Wilson* – an actress chosen by Edith Wilson herself). The other essential problem is that good drama does not always make good history, and good history does not always make good drama. Joan Allen's acting skill in the role of Pat Nixon in Oliver Stone's *Nixon* was excellent, for example, but the script's accuracy of Mrs. Nixon's character left much to be desired. Dramatic portrayals of fictional First Ladies have tended to be even more one-dimensional, usually presenting them as repressed and revengeful.

Curiously, despite the evolution of gender roles, the 1964 film *Kisses For My President*, about the first woman president's husband, played by a head-scratching Fred McMurray still seems to hold up.

But then again, there is no factual role model for a fictional First Gentleman - at least not yet.

[1] Abigail Adams to Mary Cranch, November 26, 1799, reprinted in Stewart Mitchell, ed., *The New Letters of Abigail Adams, 1788-1801* (Boston: Houghton-Mifflin, 1947), p. 218

[2] letter excerpted from Oleg Cassini, *In My Own Fashion* (New York: Simon & Schuster, 1987

[3] Elizabeth Hobbs Keckley, *Behind the Scenes, or, Thirty Years a Slave and Four Years in the White House*, 1868, reprint. (New York: Arno Press, 1968) p. 101 and Ruth Painter Randall, *Mary Todd Lincoln: Biography of a Marriage* (Boston: Little, Brown, 1953) pp. 221, 346

[4] Poppy Cannon and Patricia Brooks, *The Presidents' Cookbook*, (New York: Funk & Wagnalls, 1968) p. 80

[5] Lady Bird Johnson, *A White House Diary*, (New York: Holt, Rinehart & Winston, 1970) p. 424

[6] no date, no publication (circa summer 1881) printed matter, Lucretia Garfield biography file, container 90, Lucretia Rudolph Garfield Papers, Library of Congress

[7] In the last scenes of the film version of the Kaufman-Hart play *The Man Who Came to Dinner* (1942), actress Billie Burke answers the phone on Christmas Day only to find out that Mrs. Roosevelt is telephoning for a houseguest. "Mrs. Roosevelt? The Mrs. Roosevelt! I want you to know that my husband didn't vote for your husband, but I did. And I hope to do it again!" When she goes to fetch the departing houseguest and announces the call, the man slips on the ice and hurts his back. The very last lines of the movie are heard from the telephone by an Eleanor Roosevelt voice impersonator. "Hello? Hello? Oh dear, something must have happened!"

[8] Allan Nevins, ed., *Letters of Grover Cleveland, 1850-1908* (Boston: Houghton-Mifflin, 1933), p. 321

A. Martha Washington bookend

B. Abigail Adams pewter bust

D. Rachel Jackson ceramic miniature

C. Dolley Madison, Mary Lincoln dinner bells

E. Edith Roosevelt plate

A – R "A Gallery of Pop Culture First Ladies" Commercial products using the images of First Ladies, both contemporary to the time and those from the past have been satirical, serious, odd and artful: a bronze Martha Washington bookend, a pewter Abigail Adams bust, porcelain Dolley Madison and Mary Lincoln dinner bells, a ceramic Rachel Jackson miniature, china Edith Roosevelt and Nellie Taft plates, bisque Florence Harding, Grace Coolidge and Lou Hoover doll heads, a glass Eleanor Roosevelt whiskey bottle, an enameled Bess Truman pin, a clay Mamie Eisenhower coffee mug, a hollowed Jackie Kennedy head planter, a Lady Bird Johnson milk pitcher (with her family), Pat Nixon and Betty Ford salt and pepper shakers, a collectible Rosalynn Carter plate, Nancy Reagan and Barbara Bush slippers, a cloth Hillary Clinton stuffed doll, a plastic Laura Bush bobble-head.

H. Grace Coolidge dollhead and Lou Hoover dollhead

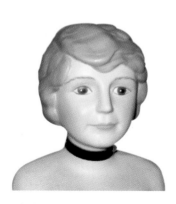

F. Nellie Taft plate

G. Florence Harding dollhead

I. Eleanor Roosevelt
whiskey bottle

J. Bess Truman lapel pin

K. Mamie Eisenhower
coffee mug

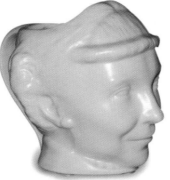

L. Jackie Kennedy head planter

M. Lady Bird
Johnson and family
milk pitcher

N. Pat Nixon and Betty Ford salt
and pepper shakers

O. Rosalynn Carter and Amy
souvenir plate

P. Barbara Bush and Nancy
Reagan slippers

Q. Hillary Clinton "Hillcare" doll

R. Laura Bush bobble-head doll